MW01088681

SNAKE-
BITE

SNAKE-BITE

Lives and Legends
of
Central Pennsylvania

JAMES YORK GLIMM

University of Pittsburgh Press

Published by the University of Pittsburgh Press,
   Pittsburgh, Pa. 15260
Copyright © 1991, University of Pittsburgh Press
All rights reserved
Manufactured in the United States of America
Printed on acid-free paper
Second paperback printing, 1994

Library of Congress Cataloging-in-Publication Data

Snakebite: lives and legends of central Pennsylvania / James
   York Glimm.
      p.   cm.
      ISBN 0-8229-3667-4 (cloth).—ISBN 0-8229-5444-3
      (paper)
      1. Tales—Pennsylvania—Susquehanna River, West
   Branch Region.   2. Anecdotes—Pennsylvania—
   Susquehanna River, West Branch Region   3.
   Susquehanna River, West Branch Region, (Pa)—
   Biography.
   I. Glimm, James York.
   GR110.P4S64   1991
   398.2'09748'5—dc20   90–49473
                                                        CIP

A CIP catalogue record for this book is available from the
British Library.

Eurospan, London

The text decorations used in this book are from *Silhouettes:
A Pictorial Archive of Varied Illustrations*, Edited by Carol
Belanger Grafton, and *More Silhouettes: 868 Copyright-Free
Illustrations for Artists and Craftsmen*, Edited by Carol
Belanger Grafton, both published by Dover Publications,
Inc.

CONTENTS

SNAKEBITE
COUNTRY, PA.

INTRODUCTION

I SOUGHT OUT THE PEOPLE IN THIS book because I wanted to know more about the people of north-central Pennsylvania, my adoptive home. Perhaps by listening to their life stories and local folktales, by collecting and writing them down, I could get deeper inside this special place, perhaps even come to feel like a native. To write a book that people in the region could identify with, that would remind them of their rich past, I could think of no better way than to let those who have lived here speak their minds, say their piece. Finally, I wanted this book to give pleasure, to make people laugh, sigh, and shake their heads, to pull them along, to inform while giving pleasure.

My deep affection for the land, the wildlife, the people and their culture made my fieldwork and writing a labor of love. Gathering materials for this book, I explored many new places and had a few adventures. I found myself tape-recording great-grandmothers in empty mansions, listening to lies in remote hunting camps, skidding down icy farm roads at midnight, bucking hay with farmers, making maple syrup with homesteaders, laying up concrete blocks with construction workers, badgering strangers to reveal the names of good storytellers, convincing informants I wasn't selling insurance or religion, and interviewing so long I forgot what I was there for in the first place.

I came to regard fieldwork as a kind of fly-fishing: I had to pick the right day to go, locate my subjects, stalk them, present the bait, hook it, and play it. When I succeeded, I took my prizes home and prepared them with loving care. As in trout fishing, the pleasures of collecting stories far outweighed the hardships, and—as you will see—the fishing was good. Make no mistake: rural people in the Susquehanna River basin do not open up easily. It takes just the right approach. Some people still won't talk to me, don't trust me. However, a playful, stalking approach helped me explore different groups in the region and get a feeling for the whole culture.

I did all of my collecting and interviewing in central Pennsylvania. Although *Snakebite* overlaps somewhat with the territory covered by my earlier book, *Flatlanders and Ridgerunners: Folktales from the Mountains of Pennsylvania,* I was mainly concerned with the central farming culture along the Susquehanna River's West Branch. I collected material in Lycoming, Clinton, Centre, Sullivan, Bradford, Tioga, Potter, Cameron, Elk, Northumberland, Blair, Snyder, Union, and Luzerne counties, along Interstate Highway 80. I did not work in the south-central—that is, the Selinsgrove-Harrisburg-Gettysburg—region at all.

The only towns of any size I visited were Williamsport, Hazleton, and Lock Haven. Williamsport, largest of the three, has about seventy thousand people with its suburbs. Small towns, farms, hamlets, wooded ridges, and large state forests make up the rest of the area. Generally, the farther north, the more rural and sparsely populated the land becomes. South of Williamsport, rising up in my own backyard, Bald Eagle Ridge reaches sixteen hundred feet and runs south for a hundred miles. Rocky, wooded ridges divide fertile and beautiful limestone valleys like Nippenose Valley, Sugar Valley, Nittany Valley, Penns Valley, and Buffalo Valley. These long valleys are quilted with dairy farms and quaint rural towns where Amish people park their wagons alongside pickup trucks on the main street. The land was settled in the 1700s before the French and Indian War, and the bigger towns like Mifflinburg and Middleburg have a settled, German flavor.

To the north, the ridge-and-valley landscape stops abruptly at the West Branch of the Susquehanna, a quarter mile wide at Williamsport. A few miles north of the river, the Allegheny Front rises abruptly to around 2,000 feet and continues into New York State. This rocky, wooded front is really an eroded plateau, but its steep ridges and valleys make it appear like rows of mountains rolling endlessly. Once the heart of a logging empire, today the northern counties in central Pennsylvania hold only a handful of people and an abundance of game; scattered dairy farms, rustic towns, state forests, and state game lands make up most of the Northern Tier.

The tranquil, even dreamy impression the region first gives belies its dynamic past. The elderly people I talked with had seen many major changes. We live in a world of such rapid, almost overwhelming change that it is tempting to feel nostalgic about a timeless past. Yet people who have lived in north-central Pennsylvania for the past eighty years have experienced wrenching social and economic disruption all their lives. In some ways the changes they saw long ago were more radical than what younger people have seen in the postwar era. The old people I talked to have experienced the amazing incursions of the railroad, the widespread use of the internal combustion engine in tractors and automobiles, electrification, the clear-cut logging of thousands of square miles, the development of coal mining, labor activism, unions and strikes, the influx of immigrants and their integration in the community, the growth and decline of the lumber industry, the sudden rise and fall of millionaires, depopulation, aviation, two world wars, influenza and measles epidemics, Prohibition, the Great Depression, the end of home births, the employment of women in factories, the phonograph, cinema, and television, and much more.

Good talkers and colorful personalities from the region, especially old-timers, were recommended to me by mutual friends and acquaintances. I have found that the following method of interviewing works best. First, I introduce myself to prospective storytellers over the telephone, sometimes calling four or five times for an informal chat before trying to set up an interview. If my subjects are nervous or evasive, as often happens, I might ask those who recommended them to call and reassure them regarding my intentions. (With three informants I am still going around this way after three years.) My last resort is to call and say, regretfully, that I must give up in my attempt because obviously they don't want to be interviewed. In many cases I am in the house taping a few hours later; it isn't every day someone asks for one's life story.

When at last I meet a new subject, I try to find a good place to listen without sitting in the informant's favorite chair. Sometime during the first hour I ease around and turn on my tape recorder—I find a small microcassette most useful and convenient— explaining that it is just an aid to my note taking. Although I tell my informants that they are being taped, they usually ignore the machine, as though it is more a toy than a tool.

As I listen, I jot notes, monitor the recorder, respond now and then, and pay as close attention as I can—doing whatever is necessary to keep the narrative rolling. I sometimes interject comments of my own if I feel my storytellers need a rest or their stories have lost direction. I try to conduct the interview like a real conversation. People do not like simply to answer questions or deliver a monologue for twenty minutes or more; they appreciate being interrupted now and then by a listener's comments because they need time to think.

Sometimes my storytellers were a little too garrulous, especially in recollecting their own lives. Thus for the autobiographical narratives in this collection, I worked through many hours of taped interviews to get a condensed version—all the while making every effort to preserve the spirit of the original.

The book presents examples of the three most

popular kinds of orally transmitted stories in this region: folktales, true stories, and autobiographical narratives. Folktales, contained in chapters 1 and 2, are anonymous fictional stories that get retold often and travel by word of mouth from place to place. Chapter 3 presents legends—stories that started out as true and gradually grew into fiction, no doubt because people just loved talking about their subjects so much that they started embroidering on them, embellishing truth with imagination. Accounts of things that really happened are given in chapter 4, tales of trouble and disaster, and chapter 5, true stories. Many older people I interviewed recalled the events of large portions of their lives; their stories are given in chapters 6 and 7.

All of the folktales and narratives recorded here were told to me. Some readers will recognize stories they have heard before; they are not all original. But a familiar tale may be told differently in central Pennsylvania. Some may even have been recorded and published before; people sometimes read a story and then return it to the oral tradition by telling it to someone. Nobody owns a good oral tale.

I thank all those who have shared with me their rich histories, their memories, and the fruits of their fancy. They have brought me a little closer to their experience and have welcomed me to the neighborhood.

1

THAT'S MY DEER
Short Folktales

BY FOLKTALE WE MEAN AN anonymous story that circulates by word of mouth. Folktales are fictional, not true; they harken back to a world of magic where deer spring up and run away with guns, where three-legged chickens outrun cars and special hogs have wooden legs. Yet the modern folktale may take a surprising variety of forms, including anecdotes and jokes.

A tale's appeal lies in its neat plot, striking characters, and artful telling. In fact, the artfulness of the narrative is everything. Listeners, especially children, don't expect a folktale to be about everyday reality—not directly, anyway. When I told a number of these stories to a group of third-graders, they knew right away the tales were "just stories," so they listened attentively, as if drawn by instinct to the core of validity at the heart of a folktale. Adults, on the other hand, may be more apt to question the usefulness of folktales. What good are they? Are they merely amusing, merely a diversion, like mediocre television?

The term *folktale* has acquired a somewhat narrow, esoteric meaning that does not reflect all the forms the genre can take. In today's culture, we most often hear folktales from friends and acquaintances in the form of jokes and riddles. Off-color anecdotes about the royal family, the president, the space shuttle Challenger disaster, or the AIDS epidemic spread like prairie fires. Such jokes may do more than amuse; they also may reflect a deeper anxiety or concern we feel about fearful or abstract issues such as incurable disease, politics, or the economy. We

2

pass jokes and stories on because they both release tension and amuse us.

Usually one can find a psychological reality at work in a folktale; its significance usually exceeds the scope of the tale. Folktales treat emotional and psychological issues by indirection, using a funny or fantastical story to make a point about aging, love, growing up, or mortality.

"That's My Deer" was overheard by one of my students in a hunting camp during deer season. One of hundreds of variants of the wounded-deer-that-didn't-die story, this type of tale has as many true variants as fictional ones. This tale also points to the problem of woods overcrowded with hunters during deer season. My student also heard "The Gun Rack," which is really about an aging man's loss of some of his vital powers—suggested by the women's laughter at the man's loss of his gun. "Meatloaf," collected by Rudy Radocaj of Stony Fork, illustrates the formula story with a good punch line. "Cats" comes from Edwin Morley, age ninety-two, of Gold, up near the New York State border in Potter County. Morley recalled tale after tale—short formulaic narratives told to him as true stories when he was a boy. These tales were probably once in oral circulation throughout the Northern Tier. "Cats," "Gifts for Dad," "A Visit to Santa," and "Door-to-Door Chickens" are folktales, while "Keeping the Peace" is a simple anecdote.

"The Right Horse," a favorite among my young listeners, has all the trappings of a formula tale. It is a variety of the "numbskull" story, one that amuses us by making us wonder how anybody could be so stupid. The man tries everything and misses the obvious. Its companion, "A Valuable Lesson," is patterned after an Aesop fable. Both were told by Tom Rosencrans, a lover of folk music who grew up in Montoursville and now teaches school in Northumberland.

"Prayer" and "A Special Hog" were told by Kermit Kerstetter of Greenburr in Sugar Valley, where the small dairy farms that went out of business in the 1960s have been bought up by the Amish. Kermit drove me down the valley to see a hog butchering at an Amish farm. I watched, fascinated, as men and women in severe black costumes from another era bustled around cutting, scalding, and draining, obeying time-honored techniques for butchering animals.

Johnny Swartz, the barber, has been working in his small Mansfield shop for over twenty years. The students called him a fascist in the sixties because he was anti-hippie and favored the United States' involvement in the Vietnam War. Today's students consider him a sage because in some ways they are more conservative than he is. Lots of good hunting and fishing talk goes on in Johnny's barbershop. "Bragging at the Barbershop" and the fish story contained within it are his.

"The Zigmall" was told by Billy Wolfe of Slate Run, where he owned and ran Wolfe's General Store for many years. The story typifies the tall tales about fantastic creatures that were popular in lumber camps. Billy was a boy when the great days of the lumber, coal, and railroad era were coming to an end, but as an old man he had not forgotten their lore.

On the surface, "Three-Legged Chickens" plays like a joke, nothing more. Underneath, however, we can easily find the theme of King Midas: when we try to perfect nature we end up destroying or losing it. This story also illustrates a rather typical farm joke in Central Pennsylvania. The late Robert Lyon of St. Marys told me this one. He would tell a joke in German and then tell it again in English— explaining, usually, "It just isn't right in English."

That's My Deer
Overheard at Hunting Camp

Kids are always in too big a hurry when they tag their deer. You should always make sure it is dead first, and then you should gut it out and then tag it. When I was fourteen I finally shot my first deer. Boy, was I proud and excited! I wanted to do everything just right. I ran over to the deer, pulled out my tag and my pencil, filled it out, and tagged the deer. I didn't want anybody claiming my deer. Only problem was this: the deer was only stunned, it wasn't dead. As I reached for my knife, the deer jumped up and ran away, tag and all. I didn't have time to reload and shoot as it ran away.

I watched the deer hop off into the woods. A few minutes later, I heard a shot. I got up and ran in the direction of the deer and the shot. That was my deer, I thought. After running a hundred yards or so, I saw a man bending over my deer. I could see he had shot it and that now it was dead. Before he could begin to dress out the deer, I yelled, "Hey, mister, that's my deer you're going to cut."

He just looked at me surprised and said, "The heck it is. I just shot this deer."

"Then how come it's got my tag on it? Take a good look for yourself if you don't believe me," I said.

Then the man looked around and found the tag on the deer. He looked up at me with an amazed look on his face and said, "Kid, if you can run fast enough to tag a deer without firing a shot, then you can have the darn thing."

The Gun Rack
A Mansfield University Student

Early one morning back in the 1970s, I was hunting along Bald Eagle Ridge on the first day of buck season. I was standing behind a tree up on the hill right where our land meets the state lands. It was so cold I could feel my breath freezing in the air in front of me. I thought to myself, "Maybe you're too old to be out hunting deer like this. Maybe you better leave it to the young men."

All I could think about was heading home where it was warm, but I had just bought this expensive new deer rifle and I knew I had better shoot a buck or at least see one. So I stayed where I was and waited in the cold. Later on, around nine-thirty, I heard some rustling, and soon four does came trotting by. Then I saw a nice big buck, a six-pointer, coming along behind them. I aimed my new rifle, shot, and watched the deer run off.

I ran out and looked where I had shot him. There was some blood on the ground, so I set off to find my prize. I took my time because I get tired easy these days, but after following the blood trail for a hundred yards I came on him. He lay in a clearing and looked dead to me. I didn't poke him or anything. I was so proud when I looked at that big rack that I just laid my rifle across the antlers like they were hanging on a wall for a trophy. Then I reached for my knife and got ready to dress it on out.

Now, just as I bent down, the deer gave a shudder and then a snort and jumped up on its feet and ran away—with my new rifle still hanging from its antlers.

So I ended up going home with no deer and no gun. When I got home, my wife was sitting there with some of her friends, and when I told them what happened I don't know whether they believed me or not, but they laughed themselves silly.

Meatloaf
Rudy Radocaj, Stony Fork

An old, established local restaurant served a specialty of the house that was pretty famous. It was a type of meatloaf that was just super good.

7

Needless to say, the old gentleman who owned the place kept his recipe a closely guarded secret. One of his longtime friends decided to find out just what the recipe was. So he needled the owner for weeks and months.

Finally, at a weak moment, the restaurant owner told his friend what he did. He told him the secret was that he put some wild meat in the meatloaf. It was rabbit.

His friend accepted that, but when he got to thinking, he realized there was no way that a person could get enough wild rabbit to feed the amount of people the restaurant fed. So he needled the owner some more. The owner was getting pretty upset by now and told his friend he did mix a little horse meat in the stuff to give it body. And now the friend persisted even more to find out just what the exact mix of this wonderful meatloaf was.

Finally the owner told him: "It's fifty-fifty for a perfect mix. One horse to one rabbit."

Cats
Edwin Morley, Gold

We always had people working on the farm up north here who were kind of slow. You gave them a decent place to live and paid them a fair wage and they would never complain. But don't ask them to do anything that required thinking, because they couldn't do it. Well, my father had a bunch of them working the place up here when I was a kid, and one time he felt the cats were getting out of hand in the barn. We always had cats around to keep the rodents down. Hodge was the name of these people. "Mr. William Hodge, I have a job for you," my father said to one of his workers. "We have too many cats in the barn and I want you to kill off three of them. I'll give you fifteen cents a cat. What do you say?"

Bill liked the sound of forty-five cents, so he said, "Sure thing, Boss. I'll just run right on down and do it now."

He was back in twenty minutes with a big smile on his face. My father said, "Well, Bill, did you do the job I asked of you?"

Bill nodded. "Yep, I sure did, Boss, just like you said."

"And how much do I owe you then, Bill?" my father said.

Bill thought for a minute, and then he said, "Ha, you can't fool me there. You owe me forty-five cents. I killed fifteen cats at three cents apiece."

Gifts for Dad
Edwin Morley, Gold

A unt Effie had to go take care of my uncle one time, so she left Uncle Arlo and their son, Merle, to take care of themselves. Now, Merle was working a lumber camp below Coudersport and he'd come home on weekends. In those days folks shared the same bunks and Merle and Arlo bunked together. First week back from camp, Merle had the logger's itch, and of course he give it to his dad.

A week or so later he came home with head lice, and again he gave them to his dad.

Next time he come home, Arlo looked at him and said, "Well, son, what did you bring me this time?"

A Visit to Santa
Edwin Morley, Gold

My uncle and aunt were shopping up in Elmira one Christmastime. They had little Edwin with them and he was about three years old and could say the darndest things. They took him to one department store to visit Santa and he told him everything he wanted for Christmas. Then they went across the street into another store and walked past another Santa Claus.

"And what do you want, my little fella?" Santa said to little Edwin.

Edwin just looked at Santa and said, "You forgot already, you old son of a bitch?"

Keeping the Peace
Edwin Morley, Gold

My dad was justice of the peace up here in Gold. Nearly everybody was poor and some folks were poorer than others and some folks just weren't

10

all there. They were always arguing about something—like trading a wife for a gun and not getting the gun—and they would come to my father to settle the darn thing.

Orey Miles and Cob Hill were at it all the time. Cob had threatened to shoot Orey and Orey was scared, so he came to Dad. Now, Dad was sick of being pestered by these two, so he just said this to Orey, "Orey, I don't think Cob is going to shoot you, but if he does, then I'll do everything in my power to make sure he's hung. Then I'll be rid of the both of you."

Then I remember Long Priscilla Burdick, they called her. She and her husband had gotten into a rumpus about something. Dad took her into his study where he had his secretary-desk and his law books and closed the door. Mom and us kids were in the kitchen. Then Priscilla started shouting and you could hear her for ten miles. One thing I remember she said was this.

My father said to her, "Do you have any children, Mrs. Burdick?"

"No," she said, "But I've been exposed a few times."

The Right Horse
Tom Rosencrans, Northumberland

Most of you young people couldn't remember when horses were used to do all the work. Let me tell you a story about what it was like when I was young and working with horses.

When horses pulled plows or wagons, they were teamed up in pairs. Every horse would work better either on the right or the left side of the plow. And the horses would get used to the same side, and if you mixed them up they just wouldn't pull right. They was left-sided and they was right-sided horses— you see what I mean?

Now, I had the finest set of horses you ever laid eyes on, but I had considerable trouble telling them apart. When I'd get those horses on the proper sides of the harness they were the best pulling team in the valley. But let me mix them up and they weren't worth a hoot. So I figured I had to find a surefire way to tell them apart.

So I cut the mane off the right-handed horse. It worked fine for a while. Then it grew back and I got confused again. So I lopped a foot off the left-handed horse's tail. Good idea, but then that grew back too. Finally I hit on a new plan—I painted a big R on the rump of the right-hand horse and a big L on the rump of the left-hand horse. After a big rainstorm, it washed off.

Well, I got smart. I'd do something that would help me know which was which forever. I measured the both of them. Now, why didn't I think of that in the first place? I asked myself. And what do you know? The left-hand horse—the white one—was two inches taller than the right-hand horse—the black one. Now I'd be sure not to mix them up if I just went by height. Pretty smart, eh?

12

A Valuable Lesson
Tom Rosencrans, Northumberland

Back in the days of horse and buggy, a father and son were traveling one day from Lewisburg to Brush Valley. The father was walking, and his son was riding on an ass. As they passed a man cutting hay, he yelled at them, "You sure look funny with the boy on the ass and the father walking."

They thought about what the man said, and the father decided that he would ride and the boy walk. It seemed the right way. But soon a woman hanging out her wash looked over the fence at them and said, "You should be ashamed, making your boy walk while you ride on the ass."

So once again they thought it over, and now they both got on the ass and rode. But a tramp sitting under a tree shook his finger at them and said, "For shame. Both of you riding on that poor donkey."

Now, they both decided to walk and give the ass a rest, but some school children pointed at them and laughed, "Look how the men walk while the ass carries nothing."

The father said, "Son, nothing we do seems to work. Let's try carrying the ass on our shoulders. Maybe people will think that is the right way to go."

So they hoisted the ass up on their shoulders and staggered down the road until they came to a narrow bridge going over a river. While crossing, they lost hold of the ass and dropped it into the river where it was drowned.

13

The father and son looked at each other for a few minutes. Then the father said, "Son there's a lesson to be learned from all our foolishness: it's just pure stupidity to try to please all of the people all of the time."

"Yeah," the son said, "and you end up losing your ass in the process, too."

Door-to-Door Chickens
Edwin Morley, Gold

The Martins used to have this meat market down near Jersey Shore. They used to make door to door sales in one of their freezer trucks.

One day Bish had been out selling his meat. He had sold all of his chickens but one. A lady came up to the truck and said she wanted to buy a chicken. Bish showed her the last one. She said that the chicken was a little small, so Bish put it back into the freezer. He moved his arm around in the freezer and brought out the same chicken again. The Bish said, "Well, how is this one?"

She looked the chicken over and said, "OK, I'll take both of them."

Prayer
Kermit Kerstetter, Greenburr

Now, Bert Homasin up to the Coudersport Pike came home drunk one night and fell into bed.

Next morning he woke up with a terrible hangover, and he called for his wife.

"Mary, Mary, oh, please come here because I think I'm going to die."

"What is it, Bert? Is it a hangover from the stuff you were drinking last night?"

"Oh, yes, Mary, please will you do something for me? Maybe a prayer would help," Bert said.

Mary got down on her knees by the side of the bed and started to pray. "Lord, please help make my husband feel better. Help him get over the awful hangover he has this morning on account of his getting so drunk last night."

"What?" said Bert as he leaped out of bed. "Mary, I asked you to pray for me, but don't tell him I was drunk."

A Special Hog
Kermit Kerstetter, Greenburr

A farmer over my way had a hog with a wooden leg, and one day I asked him why.

He said, "Well, you see, that hog is special to us here on this farm."

"What do you mean by special?" I asked.

"Well, last year the house caught on fire while we were all sleeping one night. The hog saw the fire and started whining and snorting and scraping so loud we all woke up and got out in time. Then last spring my wife was hanging clothes out to dry when the bull had gotten loose. He took one look at that laundry

15

flapping in the wind and charged my wife, but just as he came into the yard, that hog got in his way and turned him long enough for my wife to run inside. Yes, sir, that hog is something else. And last month my boy was about to run the tractor into a ditch and probably flip it over, but the hog stood by the ditch warning him. That hog is like a member of the family," the farmer said.

"But why does he have a wooden leg," I asked.

The farmer looked at me like I was real stupid and said, "Well, heck, a special hog like that, well, ya can't eat him all at once!"

Bragging at the Barbershop
Johnny Swartz, Mansfield

I've been a barber here for over forty years, and you'd be surprised at what I've seen. People who cut hair know a lot. Like this. This is a college town, right? Well the truth is that the college kids are easier to like than the locals—and I'm a local. The college kids are polite and friendly; the townspeople are always complaining about something—usually about the college kids. Anyway, I'll tell you a couple of good ones. A few years back I was cutting this fellow's hair, and he started bragging about what a great wing-shot he was. So I jumped right in and started saying what a fine grouse hunter I was too. That made two liars. So we set up a grouse-hunting trip for the following Saturday. He had a Christmas tree farm and that's where we'd hunt. Well, the day came. We hunted hard all morning and shot about thirty rounds each, but neither of us hit a thing. So I said to him, "I thought you were a good shot."

And he said, "I am, but the truth is that I needed some help trimming these trees so I can sell them in a month."

Another guy was in last year and while I'm cutting his hair he's bragging about a trout he had caught the previous spring. "Why it's a great big rainbow trout and I fight him for a half hour before I can net him, and when I measure him, he's twenty-five inches long."

About this time, the man's friend, who was sitting in the waiting chair, just couldn't take his boasting any more and said, "I hate to interrupt your story, but I was with you when you caught that rainbow trout and it was only eighteen inches long."

The guy in the barber's chair just rolls his eyes back, pats his stomach and says, "Sure, but that was over a year ago, and the way I've been feeding that trout he just keeps growing and growing."

The Zigmall
Billy Wolfe, Slate Run

The zigmall was a creature of the old lumber camps. You don't see them much any more, but they used to be all over the woods. Today when folks see them they are usually confused with flying squirrels. You see, when they travel they have a

17

webbing between their front and rear legs which lets them glide through the air like a flying squirrel. But there is a big difference.

The flying squirrel leaps from trees, but the zigmall propels itself in another way. The zigmall has a long thick tail and on the end of the tail is a large, hard rubber ball. This rubberlike ball is extremely bouncy.

To fly, the zigmall takes its tail in its front paws, swings the ball around its head faster and faster, then pounds it down on a tree stump and—*Boing!*—up it goes into the air. Then it spreads its wings and glides for forty or fifty feet.

One time, the cook in the Sinnemahoning Lumber Camp caught one of these critters and skinned it all out. The ball on the end of the tail he took and sliced up into pieces which he used to make heels for his boots.

He decided he'd try an experiment. He got up on the roof of the cookhouse and he jumped off with those special heels on.

Well, he bounced and he bounced and he bounced higher and higher. So they couldn't catch him or stop him, and by suppertime they had to put dough in the shotguns and shoot biscuits up to him to keep him from starving.

Three-Legged Chickens
Robert Lyon, St. Marys

A man was driving along a lonely rural road near Milheim one day when he noticed a chicken running alongside his car. Now, the chicken was running very fast, because the man was doing thirty-five miles an hour. So he thought he'd just speed up some and see if the chicken could keep up. The chicken passed him at fifty miles an hour, so the guy floored his car and went past the chicken at sixty-five miles an hour. But soon the chicken whizzed past him again, ran up the road a bit, and turned off onto a farm road. Then he realized what he had seen. This chicken had three legs—that explained the amazing speed.

Slowly he turned down the farm lane and drove up to a rundown farmhouse. He wanted to know more about this three-legged chicken. Then he noticed another one, a different-colored three-legged chicken, dart across the road. On the front porch sat a tired-looking old farmer. "Hello, mister," the man said. "I'm just passing through. I wonder if you could tell me anything about a three-legged chicken."

"Heck, yes, I can," the farmer said from the front porch. "We got 'em all over the place around here. Fact is, we bred 'em."

"You bred these three-legged chickens?" the traveler asked.

"Yep. You see, my wife and I and our son, Brad— well, we all like the leg on a chicken, but every time we ate one for dinner we were one leg short. So after years of fooling around with breeding and genes and such I came up with these here three-legged chickens. Yes, sir, a fat and healthy bird they turned out to be—fast, too.

"So I noticed," said the traveler. "They are the

fastest thing I've ever seen, but tell me, just how do they taste? Are they any good?"

"Well, now, there you've got me, stranger," the old farmer said. "We ain't never tasted one because we ain't never caught one."

2

THE MINNOW AND
THE MOONSHINE
Longer Folktales

L ONGER FOLKTALES CONTAIN MORE episodes and more involved plots than short tales. The distinction, however, is arbitrary: long tales can be simple, and short tales can be complex. Such stories existed thousands of years before they were written down, and scholars have suggested that fairy tales, such as those collected by the brothers Grimm, may have circulated in oral form in ancient India five or six centuries before the time of Christ.

The modern short story and the folktale are in many ways cousins: both encompass a short span, both deal with psychological complexities, and both entail a minimum of characters and events and—in most—a rigorously controlled plot. While some are realistic and particular, other folktales enchant by their timeless settings, universalized—often unnamed—characters, and repeated, formulaic patterns of action.

To the reader who says, "Hey, I have heard that one before," I say, of course, you have heard it, because it is in the oral tradition. I would be surprised if readers have not heard at least one of these stories before. As with the art short story, we enjoy the economic efficiency with which the narrative builds to a climax. Hardly a line or word gets wasted in the telling.

"The Minnow and the Moonshine," told by Marvin Mitchell, a retired forester, praises the mythical power of Prohibition whiskey. Its snappy ending works well when told aloud. George Miller told "Coon Monkey" to Rudy Radocaj who told it to me, but I suspect George first heard it from our mutual friend, the late Owen Baker, a dairy farmer. We all hunted coons with Baker and his dog Wonder up in the Wellsboro Junction area. Mike Kline, formerly a folklorist at Davis and Elkins College, collected a version of this tale from a man in prison.

Larry Miller told me "Indian Captives," and my son Jordan told a brief version of it also. Utah Phillips has used it, so it must be a well-traveled traditional tale. "The Signal" was told by Frank Schuler out at Harry Clark's in Collomsville one spring day. I had not heard this gem before and I have not heard it since from other sources. It is my favorite tale to tell to adult audiences. The absurdity of the final image and the way it ties in with local culture makes it a regional classic.

Tom Rosencrans, Rob Cook, and I had just finished a storytelling workshop for state parks interpreters at Crystal Lake in Sullivan County when a woman came up and told us "A Sicko in the Neighborhood." That was the first time I had heard the story, but since then it seems that everyone has a dead rabbit story. This complex folktale has swept over Pennsylvania in the last eight months. The story focuses on a neurotic urge to keep up appearances—unnatural behavior that creates more problems.

"If Ya Gotta Go, Start Early"—a well-traveled joke, I hear—was told to me by Jack Novak, a school principal in Mansfield. "Foxhound" was told to me by Joe Dietrich, after a day's deer hunting. Although he heard it from Don Davis, a popular storyteller, Dietrich had adopted it and had begun to invent his own details.

23

"Sandy Brown's Farm" is a composite of traditional exaggerations that I heard from Walt Campbell, Robert Lyon, Billy Wolfe, and others. I heard "The First Truck in the County" from Mark Orshaw of Milan. "Buttermilk" I collected from an itinerant Mennonite preacher, a fine talker and performer who could go on for hours. Angie Pannebaker, one of my students, made the meeting possible.

The Minnow and the Moonshine
Marvin Mitchell, State College

My friend Rob and I used to go bass fishing in the West Branch of the Susquehanna down around Muncy. For bait we used live minnows skewered with a needle with a double hook attachment out the back. Usually they worked fine, but on this day we were having no luck. We noticed an old man following us along the river as we drifted downriver. At one point he came to the edge of the river, pushed back the willows, and called out, "You boys having any luck?"

"No, no luck," we shouted back at him.

So he followed us for another fifteen minutes along the bank, and then he parted the willows again and hollered, "Want to try some of this?"

Now, we were close to the riverbank on his side, so we could both see what he was holding up—a mason jar of moonshine. It was tempting. We decided to take a break, row in to shore, and try some of this man's whiskey. Well, we sat down with this comical old guy and immediately he began to pass his jar around. The whiskey was the smoothest, strongest stuff I ever tasted. After we each had a few swigs, the old man said, "Now, what are you using for bait that you can't catch a bass out in the river today?"

"We're just using a minnow with the standard rig," I said.

"Let's have a look at him," he said. "That is the tiredest minnow I ever saw. That won't catch fish. You got to have something with fight in it, something that will look a bass in the eye."

Having said that, he reached out for the minnow already on the line and held it over the quart jar of moonshine. And taking the line just above the minnow he dropped it into the whiskey. The minnow changed in a flash: its little eyes popped open, its tail began to whip, and it started swimming quick circles around the mason jar. When he removed the minnow from the jar, it seemed to make a snap at his finger. "Go out and try this," the old man said.

Quickly I rowed out to a big hole in the middle of the river and Rob made a cast. It was just like on "American Sportsman." The minnow hit the water and went down for a few seconds, then—*Bam!*—the river exploded. A huge fish was leaping up in the air, tailwalking toward our boat and kicking up spray and foam all around. Rob's rod was bent in half and his line was humming. Luckily we had a big salmon net in the boat. After about thirty minutes of fight, he reeled the fish in and I netted it. It was a twenty-eight-inch bass, the biggest ever caught in the river here. And do you know, the minnow had that big bass right by the back of the neck.

Coon Monkey
Rudy Radocaj, Stony Fork

Now, folks down Monument way, up Beech Creek, they're big on coon hunting. Who's got the best dog and stuff. So one of the men goes away and comes back with a monkey and takes him coon hunting one night with the rest of the guys. They tree a couple of coons, the dogs do, and the men run over.

Then the guy takes out a key and unlocks the chain on the monkey's leg. See, he's got the monkey on his shoulder and the chain on the monkey's leg. He unlocks the monkey, takes out his pistol, loads it, and hands it to the monkey.

The other hunters start to run, but the man says, "Hold it, boys. This here monkey is a trained coon huntin' monkey. Don't be afraid. Just watch this. Now go up and get them coons."

With that, the monkey shinnies up the tree with the pistol in its hand. A few minutes later—*Bang!*—and a coon drops out of the tree. Then—*Bang!*—and another coon drops out of the tree. Then the monkey comes on down and hands the gun to the guy and jumps up on his shoulder.

"That's some coon monkey you got there," his friends say.

Now, a week goes by and the boys want to go coon hunting again, so they go over and ask the man if he wants to go hunting and bring his monkey and all. "No, boys, I can't go, 'cause I got to go out of town, but I tell you what. I'll let you borrow my

26

monkey and you do just like I done. Share and share alike."

So they take the monkey and pretty soon the dogs are barking like they've treed a coon and the men come over, unlock the monkey, give him the loaded gun, and send him up the tree. Well, they hear him rustling around up there, but he doesn't shoot.

"Maybe there's nothing up there."

After a while, the monkey comes down the tree. When he gets to the ground, he takes one look at the dogs and—*Bam! Bam!*—he shoots both of them right between the eyes. The men get scared and grab the gun from the monkey, lock him up, and run on home.

When their friend comes home, they return the monkey and tell him how the monkey shot the two dogs when he came down from the tree they were barking up.

"Oh, my gosh, boys," the owner said. "There's one thing I forgot to tell you about this monkey. If there's one thing he can't stand, it's a lying dog."

Indian Captives
Larry Miller, Wellsboro

It is a little-known historical fact that two of the first white explorers up the West Branch of the Susquehanna were Frenchmen named Jacques Duval and John Denier. Back in the early 1700s they befriended the Susquehannock Indians and were treated royally. But in a raid on the Susquehannock, the Iroquois captured Duval and Denier in about 1748 and dragged them over to a place near where Lock Haven is today. They were then told they would be executed, but each one could choose the way he died.

Denier was first, and he pointed to the chief's flintlock pistol. "I want to do this myself. No redskin is going to kill me," Denier said.

Then he put the gun to his head and blew his brains out. Duval watched in horror. As soon as he was dead, the squaws ran out, skinned him, and stretched his skin over a drying rack beside the skins of other animals. Not far away stood the frame of an Indian canoe. "My God," thought Duval, "they are going to use Denier's skin for the canoe."

When the chief saw that Duval understood about the canoe, he said in broken English, "White man hide make good canoe. Canoe go fast. Now, white man, how you want to die?"

Duval thought fast. Then he screamed, "A fork, you bloodthirsty savages, a fork! I want to kill myself with a fork."

Now, the Iroquois didn't use forks. Nor did any Indians, for that matter. But the chief was true to his word, so he sent out a raiding party to get a fork. In about two weeks they came back with a dozen scalps, some guns and clothes, and a silver fork.

By this time, Duval was nearly crazy. He'd been tied to a stake in the center of the village and the Indians would throw stuff at him and spit on him. So when the fork came, he was screaming and cursing them like a lunatic.

Then the chief and the braves gathered round,

28

untied Duval, stripped him, and gave him the fork. "Now you die," the chief said.

Duval took the fork. "That's right, now I die," he said, and he started jabbing his arms and legs and butt with the fork. The blood started shooting out all over the place and he just kept jabbing and laughing and screaming like a madman. The Indians looked at him with their mouths open. Then, just as he was getting too weak to jab himself any more, he screamed, "You can kill me, but you can't make a canoe out of me!"

Then he died.

The Signal
Frank Schuler, Collomsville

Over in Sugar Valley a young Amish couple were having some kind of marital problem. They had only been married a few months, but it seems they just weren't having any luck in the way newlyweds should. This all came out later, and of course everybody in these small valleys knows everybody else's business. Now, the young man's problem was this. He owned and used one of those old John Deere tractors—the kind with the nice ice-cream scoop seats. Well, he'd ride around on that tractor, get to bobbing up and down, and the urge would come over him. So he would head for home, but by the time he got home the urge had left him. And that, in short, was the whole problem.

Now, Amish hate to go to doctors, but this one

went to an old doc in Jersey Shore. The doctor
listened, shook his head, rubbed his chin, and said,
"It's a strange cure, but it's the only thing I can
think of to clear up this problem. Do you have a
hunting rifle? You do? Good. Now listen carefully
and do what I say. You take the loaded thirty-ought-
six out with you on the tractor, and when the urge
comes over you, point the gun up in the air, fire a
round, and let her come running out to you. When
she gets there, just let nature take its course."

Well, he gave it a try, tried firing the gun, and the
wife came running over the furrows and the new corn
with her long blue dress hitched up—*and it worked.* In
fact, it worked so well we could hear that gun go off at
eleven o'clock almost every day. The report from the
gun would echo through the valley. Folks would stop
and listen and smile. If you were up high, you could
look down and see the little black dot sprinting
through the hay or the alfalfa. Then we'd all go about
our business. It gave us a kind of a warm feeling to
know things were going good for them down there.

That was summer. All through fall and on into
the colder days, the shot would ring out. Then one
day the doctor happened to be over in Loganton
walking down the street when he saw the young
Amish man shuffling along, crying and looking
totally depressed. "What's wrong, young man? I
thought all your problems were over, I thought you
and your wife were doing just fine."

The young man wiped a few tears away and said to
the doctor, "Things were just fine, Doc, until
hunting season came and then my wife—well—she
run herself to death."

30

A Sicko in the Neighborhood
A Young Woman

My friend lives in a nice suburban neighborhood near Allentown. He has a golden retriever that loves to bring things home to him. One afternoon he came home and found the dog had gotten loose and brought home the neighbor's pet rabbit—dead.

Now, the people who lived right behind him were his good friends, and he knew how their kids loved this large pet rabbit. So you can imagine how horrified he was when he saw his dog chewing on the pet with its fur all covered with dirt, like the dog had dragged it in the dirt.

He didn't know what to do. He had a feeling that his friends would somehow find out his dog had killed the rabbit when the hutch door had accidently swung open, or maybe the dog had jimmied the latch trying to get at the rabbit. Right now, his friends and their kids were away on vacation. He expected them back the next day—and he was supposed to be keeping an eye on the house.

Finally he made a decision. The rabbit was dead; there was nothing he could do about that. He just didn't want them thinking he'd let his dog kill their rabbit. No, he thought, the rabbit is going to look like it died in its cage, or had a heart attack or something. My dog never touched it.

So he picked up the dirt-covered rabbit and took it to the sink where he scrubbed and washed it with detergent, hosed it down with the spray hose, and toweled it off until it was just damp. It was looking

31

better already, he thought. Finally, he got his blow-dryer and dried and combed the white fur until the rabbit looked almost alive. "They'll think it just died in its sleep," he said as he looked at his work.

Then, after it got dark, he slipped into their backyard, put the white rabbit in its hutch all natural-like, closed the latch, and tiptoed back to his own house.

Late the next day, his friends returned from their vacation. He tried not to look out the window. A few hours later, the man knocked at his door. He had a strange look on his face. When my friend asked him if they had a good vacation, he said, "Yeah, everything was fine until we got home, and that's why I'm here. We've got a sicko loose in the neighborhood and I just came over to warn you. See, our rabbit died about a week ago and we buried it in the flower bed. But some weirdo has come along and dug it up, cleaned it up and put it back in its pen."

If You Gotta Go, Start Early
Jack Novak, Mansfield

AN old-fashioned lady, always quite delicate and elegant, especially in her language, was planning a week's vacation with her husband in Florida. So she wrote a certain campground and asked for a reservation.

She wanted to make sure the campground was fully equipped, but she didn't quite know how to ask about the toilet facilities. She just couldn't bring herself to write the word *toilet* in her letter. After much deliberation, she finally came up with the old-fashioned term *bathroom commode*. But when she wrote that down, she still thought she was being too forward. So she started all over again, rewrote the entire letter and referred to the bathroom commode merely as the *B.C.* "Does the campground have its own B.C.?" is what she actually wrote.

Well, the campground owner wasn't old-fashioned at all, and when he got the letter he just couldn't figure out what the woman was talking about. That B.C. business really stumped him.

After worrying about it for a while, he showed the letter to several campers, but they couldn't imagine what the lady meant, either. So the campground owner, finally coming to the conclusion that the lady must be talking about the location of the local Baptist church, sat down and wrote the following reply:

Dear Madam:

I regret very much the delay in answering your letter, but I now am pleased to inform you that the B.C. is located nine miles north of the campground and is capable of seating 250 people at one time. I admit it is quite a distance away, especially if you are in the habit of going regularly. But, no doubt you will be pleased to know that a great number of people take their lunches along and make a day of it. They usually arrive early and stay late.

The last time my wife and I went was six years ago, and it was so crowded we had to stand up the whole time we were there. It may interest you to know that right now there is a supper planned to raise money for more seats. They're going to hold it in the basement of the B.C.

I wish to say it pains me very much not to be able to go more regularly, but it surely is no lack of desire on my part. As we grow older, it seems to be more of an effort, particularly in cold weather.

If you do decide to come down to our campground, perhaps I could go with you the first time you go, sit with you, and introduce you to all the other folks. Remember, this is a friendly community.

Foxhound
Joe Dietrich, Mill Hall

I grew up in Clearfield, but I spent lots of time on my Uncle Charlie's farm over to Snow Shoe. Now, there was a man for hunting and for dogs. Charlie lived for hunting, and he had dogs that would hunt anything. Come a nice warm wet morning with the scent hanging good, and Old Charlie, he'd whistle up his foxhounds and off they'd go—be gone all day long, too. Charlie said the Lord had called on him to hunt the fox along the West Branch. 'Course, Aunt Nellie couldn't argue with that one. Charlie didn't work much, but he was a happy man.

Now, he rented out an old sharecropper's house on the farm to a family that had been there since day one. Their name was Simon. They had lived in the old house when it had been a log cabin, and then another generation when it had been planked over and another generation when they put the roofing material on, and now they had the aluminum siding on they was still there. About eight or nine generations since settlement in the 1850s. Problem is, they had intermarried with the woodchucks, Aunt Nellie said, and run out of brains. There was Slick Simon and Molly Simon and their two kids Lem and Flem Simon—they was twins, as you can likely guess. Anyway, Uncle Charlie took them all fox hunting with him 'cause the twins could run with the dogs.

Anyway, Charlie had a foxhound he called Barlow Knife and claimed she had the best nose in three counties, and most folks round Snow Shoe weren't about to argue 'cause they had seen Barlow Knife do some amazing tracking.

One day Uncle Charlie and the Simons were taking down the old milking shed on the back of the barn when, underneath where the fieldstone foundation had been, they found a set of fox tracks in the dry dust that must have been made just before the small basement was closed up.

"Oh, that would be about forty years ago when my daddy built that shed. That's how old those tracks would be, 'cause that space has been shut up tight ever since we laid the floor," Uncle Charlie said.

"Well, now," Slick said, "Them forty-year-old fox tracks sure would be nice to set old Barlow Knife on. You don't suppose she could follow them, do ya, Boss?"

35

Uncle Charlie looked a little peeved at Slick, but he got Barlow Knife out and let her have a sniff. She nosed around a bit and looked confused.

"She can't smell a forty-year-old track," Slick said.

"Just give her a chance," Uncle Charlie said.

Just then Barlow Knife got on a scent. She wagged her tail, hopped over the foundation, and headed off across the cornfield, casting about from side to side for the scent. When she hit the cut cornfield, she started dodging from side to side, weaving in and out around nothing.

"She's lost," Slick said.

"Nope, she's just dodging the trees that were in that field sixty years ago. She's following the track, all right," Uncle Charlie said.

At the edge of the cornfield, Barlow Knife suddenly jumped high up in air, landed, then jumped again, stuck there for a second, wiggled her hind legs, and came down again. Then she headed on down over the hill and out of sight.

"What the heck was she doing there?" Slick said.

"Fences. She was jumping the two fences where the fox jumped. 'Course they ain't there no more, but they used to be. And that second one had a hole in the top where the fox must have wiggled through. That's what hung Barlow Knife up there for a second," Uncle Charlie said.

Well, they didn't see Barlow Knife that night or next day. A week passed. Then a month. Uncle Charlie was mad at himself for getting into such a stupid contest. He figured Barlow Knife followed the track across Interstate 80 and got run over or into one of them new federal dam projects.

"Poor Barlow Knife," he said. "It's all my fault."

Well, one rainy night a month and a half after she disappeared, Uncle Charlie got a call from the police department in Harrisburg. They had checked the name and address tag on Barlow Knife and, yes, the dog was alive and well.

The police sergeant said, "Yessir, we got your dog right here. It seems she tripped the alarm system in the back of an old second-hand shop downtown. We thought it was a robbery, but we were happy to find nothing more than your dog in the back of the shop rummaging through some old clothes. Don't know how she got in."

"What was she after?" Uncle Charlie asked.

"Well," the sergeant said, "When we found her she was chewing on an old red fox stole. Happy as can be. Now, do you want us to ship the dog back to you?"

"How much will it cost?" Uncle Charlie asked.

"It will cost about ninety dollars to fly the dog into Clearfield," the policeman said.

Uncle Charlie thought for a minute. Then he said, "How much does the owner want for the fox stole?"

"What? Oh, well he's right here. He said you can have it for twelve dollars," the policeman said.

"OK, then," said Charlie, "Just send the fox stole C.O.D. to me up here and just let the dog go."

Sure enough, a few days later the mailman came walking up the street carrying a box with a fox stole in it and following just a few feet behind was none other than good old Barlow Knife—still on the track of the fox.

37

Sandy Brown's Farm
Walt Campbell, Robert Lyon, Billy Wolfe,
and others

I never knew how steep some of the land was in Pennsylvania until I started road hunting for turkeys. One day around Carroll I stopped my car when I saw a farmer lying in the middle of the road. I jumped out, helped him up and asked him what happened.

"I just fell out of my farm," he said. Then he pointed up in the air—I mean almost straight up—and there she was—a hillside of corn almost straight over my head. So we climbed hand over hand up to his farm.

"This here's the lower forty. It gets steeper up above," the farmer said.

And it was steep: time we got to the top of the farm, we could look down the chimney of the farmhouse and see what the missus was making for dinner. Sandy told me how he had to plant the corn by shooting it into the mountainside with a breechloader and how it grew out the other side of the ridge. He said they had to tie the pumpkins to the cornstalks to keep them from rolling down the mountain. In the fall they would open the cellar doors, shake the apple trees, and the apples would just roll right in.

All the cows on his farm had two long downhill legs and two short uphill legs. Of course, they weren't much for turning around. Sandy's dog had to dig a place to sit down and bark. This dog loved

38

to flush grouse in the woods. Grouse up there laid square eggs so they wouldn't roll downhill.

One day I was riding Sandy's horse down a real steep part of the hill when I felt something warm on the back of my neck. You know what happened? That hill was so steep that when the horse pooped it went on down the back of my neck. That's steep.

I went up to Sandy's farm a lot and I got to know the Browns real well, but the better I got to know them the stranger they seemed. Sandy's daughter Cora was the vainest girl I ever met. She was always looking at herself in the mirror. Fact is, she spent so much time at the mirror that if you wanted to look at yourself you had to wait for fifteen minutes until her reflection faded. She wasn't pretty at all, to tell the truth. She was downright ugly. Cora had *ugly* she hadn't even grow'd into yet. She was so ugly that with her buck teeth she could eat an ear of corn from the other side of a picket fence. One day the boys got her to stand in the cornfield; the crows took one look at her and brought back last year's corn. Now, you're talking *ugly*.

Sandy's son Wilmer was different. He was the quickest kid in the county, maybe three counties. He was so quick he could pitch and catch at the same time. He could shut off the light and jump into bed before it got dark. He could jump over his own shadow. One time he shot at a deer and ran after it so fast that he creased himself with his own bullet. Trouble was, all that darting about made him so skinny he fell through a hole in the seat of his pants and damn near strangled himself.

Sandy's farm was so high up that it would get cold real fast. One afternoon a whole mess of geese and ducks came cruising in to the pond. We figured we'd jump them early next morning and have some good shooting, but it got so cold that night that the pond froze clear through before the ducks and geese could get out. They were frozen to the pond, so when we jumped them they flew off with the whole pond.

That same winter it got so cold that when we'd go out to milk the cows and take our warm hands out of our gloves and put them on the cows' teats they'd turn around and say, "Thank you, thank you."

Headlights froze on people's cars, train whistles froze, and sunlight froze on the sidewalks. Now, country people ain't stupid. What they did with the headlights was cut the high beams off with a hacksaw, cut them up small and put them in the freezer. Hell, they used them for flashlights all summer long.

Oh, I've seen some other strange things when it got cold. I've seen a crow's shadow freeze to the snow and fix that crow in the air for three days. One day it was so cold I saw two beagles put jumper-cables on a rabbit to get him started. That's *cold.*

The First Truck in the County
Mark Orshaw, Milan

This took place back in the days when automobiles were just coming into use. Only just a few people, mostly the rich, had cars, Model Ts, and they would chug through Milton raising a ruckus with the horses and chickens and pigs that people had back then. Lots of people wanted the automobiles banned from the town. Said they were bad for business, bad for health. Chinky Latner was one of the strongest antiautomobilisters—that's what they called themselves.

Trouble was, when you saw one of Mr. Ford's cars, after the initial shock wore off, you wanted one for yourself. Chinky swore he'd never buy an automobile, that he'd die driving his team and wagon. Then Ford came out with a light pickup truck. "All bets are off," Chinky said. "I said I'd never by a car, but I didn't say nothing about a truck. Now, that's a horse of a different color."

So Chinky fell ass-over-tincups in love with the Ford truck down at Dincher's. He dug into his secret milk can and he went to the bank and he bought a brand new Ford light pickup truck. He studied up on the truck and treated it better than anything he ever had. It was the first pickup truck in the county.

Now, one day Chinky was bringing a big load of chickens to the depot. He was selling them for broilers and he had cages of them piled up high on his little truck. Marcy Hicks saw him do it first: while he was driving down the country road into town, she saw him stop the truck, jump down, go around back and pick out a long chunk of two-by-four. Then she saw Chinky lay into the tailgate with that two-by-four. That's right. He just beat the tar out of the back of his new truck. And he did it every half-mile all the way into Milton because

41

everybody on the farm road saw him do it. They were all on the same party line, you see.

Finally, as Chinky was getting in close to Milton, Buzzie Clapp, the town cop, started tailing Chinky. The next time Chinky got out to beat the tailgate, Buzzie was there waiting for him. "Chinky," he said, "it's probably none of my business at all, but I understand you've been wholloping the daylights out of your new truck since you left home, and lots of folks, me included, are wondering just what in the devil you are doing?"

Chinky already had the two-by-four out and ready like a baseball bat. Suddenly he looked up at Buzzie surprized. "Why I thought it was obvious what I'm doing. This here truck is a half-ton pickup, right?"

"Right," Buzzie said.

"Well, I'm overloaded. I've got a ton of chickens on this truck, and it can only hold half a ton, so I'm trying to keep the other half up in the air until I get to market."

Buttermilk
An Itinerant Mennonite preacher, Mainesburg

Back in the old days, folks used to use a churn to make butter. I know you've seen them in museums. The churn was shaped like a long wooden bucket with a stick called a dasher coming out the top. You'd just slosh it up and down until the butter would come. What didn't go into butter was

42

buttermilk and they saved that and used it for baking or just to drink.

Now, back in the 1920s Bill Morris was a farmer over in Milton with a reputation for making good whiskey. Of course, that was illegal back then during Prohibition. One day while Bill's seventeen-year-old daughter Sally was making butter, she began to think about her father. Bill Morris told her he was cutting telephone poles for the phone company up on Bald Eagle Mountain. He would leave every day for the mountain, but he would carry only a shotgun, not an axe or saw. Sally knew a man can't cut timber with a gun.

"What's Dad doing up there on the mountain?" she asked her mother.

"You just mind your own business," her mother said.

Later, while Sally was making butter pads with flowers on them, her father called to her, "Sally, I'm going into town. Now you help your mother while I'm gone and I'll bring you home something nice."

She noticed he was loading some runty sour apples into the truck.

"Daddy, what are you doing with those sour apples?" she asked.

"Oh, something might come up. Now I've left something up on the hill a ways. You come and sit here and don't let anybody get near this truck. I'll be right back," Bill said.

As soon as she sat down on the tailgate of the pickup truck, curiosity got the best of her. She raised up the burlap bags covering the apples and found two five-gallon stone jugs with cork stoppers. She pulled

43

out one stopper and took a whiff—moonshine. Her father was making whiskey for Prince Farrington again. "I hate to think of Daddy breaking the law," she said to herself.

She thought about how hard things were on the farm. Bill Morris had countersigned a banknote for a friend and then the friend had run off, so Bill now had to pay. Disease had killed off most of the hogs and fire had burned down half the barn. Sally was the oldest of five children, too. She knew why he was making moonshine, but she hated to think of the family living on money made illegally. And the more she thought, the more she decided to do something about it. Her father was a kind, good man and she didn't want to see him go to jail.

Two hours later, Bill Morris pulled up to a gas station in Loganton. This place was the latest drop-off place for moonshine on its way to Prince Farrington. The Prince bought whiskey from local moonshiners, blended them together, and bottled it under the label White Mule. Bill was hoping to unload his liquor and get back home. When the attendant came out, Bill said, "Want to buy some apples?"

"Not today," the attendant said.

"I got something in here better than apples," Bill said.

"Oh yeah. Don't tell me you been boiling the copper kettle at night," said the attendant.

"I got to do something, because the sheriff is about to sell me out. I promised to pay on a note if Josh Briggs defaulted, and he took off for Florida a month ago," Bill said.

44

"I'm sorry to hear it," the man said.

"My wife and daughter are dead set against it, but I don't have any choice," Bill said.

Then the man looked at Bill and said, "Look, I got orders from the Prince not to buy any whiskey today because we are expecting a big raid."

While he was talking, a car pulled up and the attendant went over. Soon he came back to Bill and said, "Look, there's a guy over there who wants to buy some moonshine. You dare try sell it to him?"

Bill thought for a minute; then he said, "Send him on over because I'm selling."

So the man got out and walked over to Bill and just looked at him. Bill smiled and said, "I've got the purest, whitest stuff made from corn—they call it white mule."

"How much is it?" the stranger asked.

"Now it costs a lot to make it, but I'll let you have it for ten dollars a gallon. I've got two gallons of the stuff," Bill said.

"That's a lot of money, but it sounds all right to me," the man said as he handed him a ten-dollar bill.

"Do you want me to put it in the car for you?" Bill said.

"No," the man said, "just let it sit because you are under arrest."

And with that, he pulled out a gun and a badge and told Bill to put his hands up in the air. Bill was so mad he started cussin' at the revenuer and started coming at him.

"Stay where you are, old man," the man said. "You made one mistake today; don't make another.

45

You came out here and made the deal all by yourself, so you are under arrest."

By now the attendant came over and tried to calm Bill down. "Take it easy, it's only your first offense. Besides, they have to have some evidence."

"Shut up and get me a glass," the lawman said to the attendant as he started rummaging in the truck. "That moonshine is right in here."

When the attendant returned with a glass, the revenuer had one of the jugs ready, and placing the glass under the top, he poured out a thick white liquid. "What the hell is that?" he said as he finished pouring.

As soon as he saw the white, Bill knew what had happened. Sally had poured out the whiskey and put buttermilk in its place. "Looks like buttermilk to me, Mister. Ain't no law against that. Thanks for the ten dollars," said Bill as he pocketed the man's money.

"Listen here, old man, you wouldn't have hauled that milk all the way down here for nothing. You try selling whiskey again and next time I'll nail you," the revenuer said.

"Mister," Bill said, "there isn't going to be a next time. My moonshining days are over."

After a few minutes, they all got to laughing about what had happened, and even the revenue man saw the humor in the situation. Then Bill decided to drive on into town and buy Sally something as a reward for getting him off like that. When he got to town, one of the bankers stopped him on the street to tell him that his deadbeat friend Josh Briggs had inherited a cattle ranch out in Wyoming and had paid off his debt and all the payments Bill had made

46

for him. Josh had a substantial refund coming. He ran to the bank and picked up the money—with interest.

With over two hundred dollars in his pocket, he headed down the street a happy man with only one thing on his mind. He was thinking he'd take his wife and Sally to the square dance, but first he was going to buy Sally the nicest dress in town.

3

PADDLEFOOT, THE PRINCE, AND THE NUMBSKULL
Local Legends and Superstitions

L EGENDS TAKE SHAPE WHEN
storytellers attribute awesome significance
to unusual local phenomena, events, and
personalities. A legendary figure is born
when storytellers begin to endow local characters with
qualities larger than life—they become heroes,
heroines, and villains. The hero has miraculous
healing skills, the heroine can shoot a deer a mile
away, the villain laughs as he watches the loggers
drown. In episodes like these, oral history crosses over
into folktale and becomes legend. It isn't characters,
remarkable deeds, or weird events alone that are the
sources of tales—although people who become
legends, like Prince Farrington, often are truly
extraordinary. The storytellers and believing listeners
raise these characters and strange episodes to
legendary levels. They keep them alive and make
them grow and change, because these embellishments
on the facts meet personal and community needs.

In U.S. folklore, Davy Crockett became the most
popular subject of legend. Thousands of tall tales
sprung up around this real-life woodsman and hunter
who served under Andrew Jackson, was elected to
Congress, and died at the Alamo. During the long
period of westward expansion, the young country
enjoyed hearing tales about Crockett and other
heroes who embodied the rough-and-tumble vitality
and splendid marksmanship of the frontiersman.

The stories presented in this chapter are miniature
versions of that larger tradition. Their protagonists
and events are known only locally, yet within a
limited area they have a real immediacy and
importance. Few people outside of Clinton and

Lycoming counties have heard of Prince Farrington, but to those who have, his fame is great. The more local an oral tale is today, the more likely it is to be the product of a true folk process. The more widespread a character's renown, the more likely it is to be a media creation.

When we hear of the exploits of a regional hero or villain, or an account of some quasi-supernatural event, we can be reasonably sure that something like these episodes actually happened—they have just grown larger than life. The legend flourishes in an area because it affirms the psychological needs and social values of the community. Understandably, people usually stop telling local legends after the era of a hero has passed. You can readily collect Prince Farrington stories along the West Branch if you ask for them, but they are not told spontaneously anymore. So the most authentic protagonists of Pennsylvania folklore are regional, small-town heroes.

"Danger in the Mines," comes from John Myers, whose coal-mining hometown of Hazleton is surrounded by miles of slag heaps, bony piles, and tipples. (Today deep open-pit mines have replaced shaft mines.) Growing up and playing near the abandoned mine shafts and air holes was common for many Wyoming Valley kids. The eerie landscape of the strippings and shaft areas gave rise to many stories.

Bob Wagner, who works at the Nippenose Valley Elementary School near Oval, grabbed me after a talk I gave to the schoolchildren. Superstitious as well as a good storyteller, he took me to a window that looked out on this magnificent valley and began to point out haunted farmhouses. Later I visited him at his home where he told me "The Phantom Dog," "The Baby's Ghost," and "McElhattan Falls."

The wild story "Shoot Me" was told by Rudy Radocaj of Stony Fork. I have also heard the story from another source, now forgotten, but I have no doubt that the events happened. Confrontations over deer— who shot what—are common. In "Shoot Me" the tension between ridgerunner and flatlander is stretched to the breaking point; after the explosion clears, the ridgerunners win on all counts. If the New Jersey guys had won the deer and routed the ridgerunners, I never would have heard the story—it never would have been told, except perhaps in New Jersey.

Clifford Bowersox told me the basically true story of Mose Booney, which I later heard in two almost identical variations. Mose was a famous hunter on Jacks and Shade mountains—ridges that stretch northeast-southwest all the way down to West Virginia. These nearly two-thousand-foot-high ridges blocked the westward movement of many early settlers. Legendary elements in the Booney story include his prowess as a hunter, his cryptic prediction of his own death, and the bandanna he ties to a tree.

Paddlefoot Khyler, so named because of his giant feet, impressed Howard Kisner as a boy. Kisner grew up to become a state trooper and sheriff. He feels fortunate that he shot at many a man but never hit one. Kisner also told me about "Rifle-Eye Smith" and "Cougar Hollow." Veris Metzger told about "Hoot the Mountain Numbskull."

I include a story from Dick Sassaman about one of the storytellers in this book—Norm Erickson, who has already become something of a living legend because of his strength, his humor, his compassion, and his ability to stand up to bureaucracy and do things his way. Perhaps readers can find origins of his legend in some of Norm's own stories, included in chapters 4 and 5.

A recurrent legendary character is Prince Farrington of Jersey Shore, who came to the area from North Carolina. Prince was a famous moonshiner during the Prohibition period who really knew how to make good corn whiskey. Everyone who tasted his "white mule," from judges to lawyers to policemen, said his whiskey was the best they had ever tasted. Confiscated goods never got destroyed. Instead, they just "evaporated"; the law enforcement people took it home. Prince was hounded and persecuted all his life after the repeal of Prohibition by the very people who once drank his liquor. He is reported to have said, "My only crime was making good whiskey." Some years ago, the *National Geographic* magazine published a photo essay on the West Branch region that highlighted "the Prince" and his daughter Gladys— who until recently ran the Antique Tavern in Jersey Shore. These Farrington stories were told by George Porter, Warren Searfoss, Kenny Crosser, and others.

Danger in the Mines
John Myers, Hazleton

When I was a kid the remains of the deep-pit mines were just a few hundred feet from my backyard. The entrances to the played out mines gaped nearby while iron plates and barbed wire warned of ventilation shafts falling thousands of feet to the tunnels below. It was a dangerous place for a kid and therefore irresistible. Although the mines were fenced off and sealed up, we kids would play in the shafts and drop rocks down the bottomless air shafts. Sometimes we would hear of an accident in a nearby town and avoid the mines for a week or so, but soon we would be back. To scare us, my grandfather used to tell stories about what would happen to us if we went near the mines. Because he had been a miner and knew all about working underground with a lamp on his head and a pick in his hands, we listened carefully to what he said. Of course, he would doctor his tales up to make them more exciting, but then we believed everything. I remember a few of those stories. One of them was about a man named Jake.

Jake worked hard for many years, so when he reached fifty, the coal company took him out of the mines and made him a supervisor. But Jake missed his buddies down in the hole, and one day he decided to make a surprise visit to the men down in a deep mine. So he took an elevator down the shaft, and when he got to the level he wanted he began to walk down a long stretch of the mine. He had gone about three hundred yards without seeing or hearing a thing when suddenly—*Boom!*—a gigantic explosion knocked his feet out from under him, lifted him in the air and up a shaft and right out into the light of day. But when he emerged from the mine into the daylight he suddenly disappeared, blown away by the explosion.

You see, Jake had been walking near an air shaft when they dynamited this section of the mine. The blast lifted him right up the air shaft. Somehow, after that, he vanished. They found his hat and shoes and that's all. Today, along the stretch of road that connects Tamaqua and Pottsville, they say you can see something walking along the highway at night—you can see a pair of boots stepping along in the dust and above the boots a hat bobbing from side to side. People believe Jake's ghost walks along, looking for the rest of his clothes.

My grandfather told another story about seven miners who worked together at a place called the Moley Dam. As a team, these men worked deep under the ground. One day, after a huge section of the rock face they were working on caved in, an object fell out before them as big as a pumpkin—a huge chunk of pure gold. They took a solemn oath to tell no one, not even their wives. They hid the gold in the wall of the mine and left. That night and every night afterwards, one of them stood secretly on guard. Every week they would meet in the mine, take out the gold, and admire it.

One night three of the men planned to steal the gold. They slipped in by another shaft and uncovered the treasure. But the four other men had grown suspicious and followed the three. When they caught the three men with the gold, they shouted and began fighting with them. Whether the mountain was angry or the sound of the fighting caused the cave-in nobody ever knew, but the seven men in the deep mine shaft were buried forever. Today, in the woods nearby, their ghosts watch for intruders who would steal their gold.

55

Grandad told that story to keep us away from the Moley Dam, a deep pool of water caused by the cave-in that killed the seven miners. This next story, though, used to scare me the most.

Holes in the earth that went straight down the mine shafts thousands of feet below were called air pockets. Because the openings got bigger over the years, and because they were just plain dangerous to be around, they were always fenced in, sealed up, or blocked off. As kids, we thought it smart to sneak in to a section of air pockets on a hot summer day. When we got older we'd bring a case of beer and hang out at night by these holes in the earth. You see, air pockets pulled air out of the mines and caused fresh air to come in through the shaft. The air coming out these vents came from deep down in the mines and in summer was incredibly cool, like air from a giant air conditioner. That's why we hung around them.

One day a man named Ducky, a man with no family, no friends, and no money, wandered out of town towards the mines. Ducky wanted to escape the heat, find a friend, and sit down and share the bottle of whiskey he had in his hand. Soon he had crawled under the fences and past the danger signs out into the mine-shaft area. And just as the sun was going down, he could feel the cool air rushing at him from one of the air pockets. Settling down beside a jet of cool air, Ducky leaned back on a rock and took a drink from his bottle. "Now, if only I had a friend to share this with," Ducky thought.

Soon he fell asleep. Sometime during the night Ducky realized someone was calling to him in his

56

sleep. Slowly he opened his eyes and sat up, fully awake. Out in front of him a figure stood between two rocks waving to him. A fuzzy yellow glow surrounded the figure and Ducky began to think one of his old miner buddies wanted to talk to him. "Hold on a minute, Jack, I'm coming, just wait till I get this bottle," Ducky said.

Happy now, Ducky stumbled across the tipple toward the image of his friend. As he got closer it seemed to fade, flicker, and shift position. Turning to follow the wispy specter, Ducky took five steps and walked straight over an air hole. His scream echoed in the hot summer night as he fell a thousand feet to his death.

Today, kids growing up near the old mines know that Ducky will try to lure them out over the air holes. He wants someone to talk to because he is so lonely. This and the other stories were told to kids to keep them away from the mines. I hope I do not live near the mines like my parents and grandfather. That's why I'm going to college, so I can get a good job and get out of the anthracite region. If ever I live near the mines, though, I will tell my kids the same stories.

Phantom Dog
Bob Wagner, Oval

An old couple over in Pine had decided to give Jake one of their dogs because his had died, so the boy walked out of his house and over to the scale

57

yards and then over the railroad bridge that used to go over the West Branch. Then he hiked down the tracks to where these people lived. Jake was excited about getting the dog, but he stayed too long thanking the old couple who didn't want him to leave. Finally, when he left it was almost dark.

The dog trotted right beside him as he walked along the tracks next to the river. Suddenly the dog stopped and wouldn't move. It started whimpering and shivering. Jake looked up to see what was frightening the dog. A white fog was rising from the river now in the dusk. Twenty yards ahead of him was a huge white dog with no head walking across the tracks. Jake could see it was a ghost as clear as can be.

He picked up the dog and ran home. He was scared out of his wits. He told his mother and father what had happened. Then his mother told him that others had seen ghosts over there near the graveyard. She told him that a man had been hung there many years ago. He had been accused of committing a murder, but many said he was innocent. His ghost still walks, sometimes as a deer, sometimes as a man, sometimes as a dog—but always without a head.

The Baby's Ghost
Bob Wagner, Oval

No one would buy the old farmhouse in the Nittany Valley around Pleasant Gap. It was supposed to be haunted. The farmhouse proper was made of fieldstone with a big chimney and windows set back in the stone. The caretaker of the place kept it trimmed up nice for the owners who lived in Florida. They kept trying to sell it, but nobody would even look at it. Word got around that the place was haunted by the ghost of a baby that had been killed there.

One day, a couple from Philadelphia with lots of money drove by the farmhouse. It was an early fall day, and the valley was filled with fruit and corn and hay and honey. When they saw the farmhouse and the loaded apple trees and the creek running through the pasture, it was love at first sight. To keep the price down, they arranged with a local attorney whom they knew to buy the place cheap.

One month later, they were moving into the stately old home. They planned to live there on weekends, vacations, and holidays. One weekend early in October, the woman was out by the pond cutting some cattails when she heard a baby crying. She turned to look and realized it was coming from the house. Her husband was in town at the time, so she walked right into the house and called out, "Hello." She was thinking that maybe some neighbors were stranded on the road, that they had a baby and had come right on inside because they needed a lift. But no one was downstairs. She followed the crying upstairs. It seemed to be coming from the tiny bedroom they called the baby room. When she got there, the crying stopped.

She told her husband about it, but of course he didn't make anything of it until a few days later when he too heard the crying from the basement. Then they had to face the truth. Their house was really haunted

59

by the ghost of a child. Sometimes they would hear the crying at odd hours—like in the middle of the night, or in the late afternoon. It was not a frightening sound. They agreed on that. It was as if the child wanted something from them, but they didn't know what it was. They had no children themselves.

It is hard to deal with such a thing. You don't want to tell too many people because they might think you are off your rocker. Of course, all the local people knew there was something wrong with the house; they were just waiting to see what was going to happen. Finally the couple asked their lawyer friend to find out if anything strange had ever happened in the house. He went to the sheriff, to the old judge, to the county records and to a couple of old-timers in the area. Then he reported back to the couple.

The news was shocking to them, but they both understood immediately. The lawyer told them that a small child had disappeared from the house eighty years ago. There was an official investigation, but nothing came of it. Immediately the couple got the state police to come out; they hired some men to tear down walls under the cellar stairs. And the police and the workers and the lawyer could hear the crying as they worked. After the men broke down a wall which appeared newer than the rest of the cellar wall, they found a pile of rags, and inside the rags they found what they knew they would find—the bones of an infant.

This child had died over eighty years ago. Perhaps it died of disease or abuse, perhaps it was murdered. They would never know. They gave the child a real burial and everyone in the neighborhood came to the funeral. You can see the grave in the cemetery in

Pleasant Gap. Don't expect me to tell you the name on the headstone. That would be unlucky. Anyway, a proper burial was all the baby's ghost wanted. After that, there was no more crying in the farmhouse.

McElhattan Falls
Bob Wagner, Oval

This story tells how the ghost of a young man came to haunt the falls at McElhattan Creek. Back in 1894 a handsome young fellow from Sugar Valley was working in a brickyard over in Sunbury. All week he would work there and stay in a boarding house in town, but every Friday he would jump on the train to Williamsport and Lock Haven and head for home. He would get off at McElhattan and hike through Pine and on over the mountain to Loganton. In good weather the walk was pleasant, but in winter it was another matter.

One bitter cold Friday afternoon in December of that year, Harry hopped off the train in McElhattan and went right to the grocery store to buy bread. The day had started bright and sunny enough, but the temperature was dropping and the sky had clouded up. A light dusting of snow danced through the last light of day. The store owner knew the young man and knew what was going on in his heart. "You better stay here, Harry. It's gonna snow bad. I think we're going to have a blizzard. She'll wait for you. You can see her in the morning when it's light and the storm passes."

61

"No, thanks, Mr. Toombs, this is nothing. I've just got to get up the road a few miles and see her. It's been a whole week. I'll just hurry up to the falls. From there it's only two miles to the camp," young Harry said.

Mr. Toombs urged him to stay, but Harry stepped out into the worst blizzard of the decade and trotted up the road leading into the mountains.

Five miles up the mountain road Harry's sweetheart, Mary, a cook at a lumber camp, waited for him as she did every Friday night. He would stop on his way home to visit with Mary, and she would fix him a meal. Then they would sit and talk together. For two years now they had been sweethearts; in the spring they would get married. So when she saw the wind whipping snow into deep drifts she prayed he would stay in McElhattan. She talked to the loggers about Harry, and they all said, "He wouldn't try it. He'll stay down below in town. We'll help you look for him next morning. He'll be all right."

As the loggers lay in their bunks that night, they heard the wail of the storm. It was worse than they expected. When ten loggers left next morning they insisted she stay behind. After a blizzard passes through, the world is white and cold and the sunlight glints off everything sharp and hard. Parts of the road were blown clear and parts were waist deep. Three miles down they came to the falls. "If he's not here, then he must be all right," one of the men said.

Then they saw just the heel of his boot sticking out of a drift under a great hemlock. He had frozen to death. They carried him like a block of ice downhill, away from the camp to the store at McElhattan. None of them could bear to think of bringing Harry's body to Mary at camp. But two days later, while his relatives were taking the body over to Sugar Valley by sled, she came out and uncovered the body and looked for the last time into his frozen face.

That was almost a hundred years ago, yet I have heard people say that during winter storms you can hear Harry's cries for help coming from the road by the falls and Mary's calls to Harry from the camp up on Bald Eagle Mountain.

Cougar Hollow
Howard Kisner, Montoursville

Folks come up to me when I'm up in camp in Cougar Hollow and say, "You know how this hollow got its name?"

"Tell me," I say.

And then they explain, "They call it Cougar Hollow because the loggers found a big mountain lion up here—used to call them "painters"—and they tracked him in the snow with dogs and hunted him down and shot him and skinned him out and wore the hide for jackets."

"Is that a fact?" I say.

"Yessir, that's the real story behind Cougar Hollow," the fellow tells me.

"It sure is interesting," I say.

I don't tell people the truth about the hollow, because I don't think they would even believe me. It would spoil their weekend if they did, anyway. These outsiders who come up here might not always go

63

back to Philadelphia or New Jersey with a turkey or
a buck or a string of trout, but they bring home their
stories of local lore and tell all their neighbors about
the wild places they visited in Clinton County. So I
just let it alone.

But just between you and me, here's the real truth
of it. This hollow was first settled by a Civil War
veteran named Charles Kuglar. He was a trapper,
and I have seen his 1862 Colt revolver. He moved
up here after the war was over. He came from Enola,
near Harrisburg. After he died the state bought up
his land. That was in 1928. They paid three dollars a
square acre for it. This was the Twenty-eighth
District and it was still called Kuglar Hollow until
some young forester came around. He must have
been given the job of naming every stream and
hollow. His name was Lawrence, and he decided
that Kuglar wasn't a good enough name, so he
changed it to Cougar Hollow. Ever since then, every
flatlander who comes up here has been telling cougar
stories about the place.

Shoot Me!
Rudy Radocoj, Stony Fork

When a flatlander buys a piece of land, the first
thing he does is post it. That's why when that
bunch of guys from New Jersey bought two hundred
acres up on Slide Mountain we knew there was going
to be trouble. See, that's our favorite hunting spot.
Our families have been driving deer up there for over

a hundred years, and we weren't about to stop because of some guys from New Jersey.

Anyway, there's a story in this if you want to listen. Here's what happened. I remember it was 1976—the Bicentennial—because we had to fight for what was rightfully ours.

After they paid somebody to fix up the cabin, the Jersey guys started coming up on weekends to raise hell in our backyard. They'd drink and tear around on all-terrain vehicles and shoot thousands of rounds into the hillside for target practice. When the sun went down, they were out spotlighting deer on everybody else's land. Later they would go into the bars and try to pick up our local women by buying them mixed drinks and dancing with them. And the girls were saying things like, "Ain't them Jersey guys cute?"

A week before buck season, they went around and posted their land. This made local guys like Les Leski, Boz Bubazyk, and Bubba Kerjeski boiling mad. They decided they were going to hunt where they always hunted: the newly posted land all around Slide Mountain.

On opening day, seven of us started out on the edge of the posted land. At first light, we moved in. It wasn't seven-thirty when I heard Boz and Bubba each shoot twice off to my right. I went over and each of them had a buck. The flatlanders were driving the deer right into us and we were picking them off. We dragged the two deer back to the road and then went back in. Les was looking for the Jersey guys more than the deer, it seemed.

Then we heard shooting up ahead. The Jersey guys

must have been driving right toward us and shooting straight ahead. Of course, they didn't expect anybody to be there. We hit the dirt and all was quiet.
That's when Les must have seen the ten-point buck ghosting through the hemlocks. The big old buck knew he was caught between two drives and he was slipping away. Then I heard Les shoot and yell, "I got him!"

I could hear the wounded deer stumble and run down the hill. Les and Boz and Bubba and I took off after the deer, following a heavy blood trail. After a minute or two, we heard ten, fifteen, maybe twenty shots right below us. We heard bullets whistling over our heads. The Jersey Army had struck.

"Those dirty bastards," Les said.

Together we walked into a clearing and saw a dozen Jersey guys standing around the dead buck. Their wild shooting had turned the fine animal into hamburger. Les walked right up to the deer and started taking off his license to tag it. "That's my deer, get out of my way," Les said.

"The hell it is," said a big, mean-looking guy with a heavy Jersey accent. "We all shot it, didn't we boys?" And besides, what are you doing on our land? We're going to have you arrested and prosecuted. You hillbillies think you can run all over posted land? You're wrong."

Meanwhile, Les was ignoring him. He was taking out his license and starting to put the tag on. He was getting out a pen to fill out the tag.

The Jersey guys looked mean. They didn't look like hunters but more like thugs. Some were fat and unshaved and wore snowmobile suits. They all carried cheap new guns and wore boots made in Korea. They carried hot seats and whiskey flasks, while fillet knives in sheaths and walkie-talkies hung by their sides. I began to get scared. Then the big guy pointed his gun down at Les and flicked off the safety.

Everything got real quiet. Les kept on writing. Then the flatlander nudged him with the barrel of the gun and said, "Buddy, get away from that deer and get off my land or I'll shoot you."

Les just stood up, looked him in the eye and said, "Come on, you asshole! Shoot me! Shoot me! *Shoot me!*"

The flatlander looked at Les like he was a madman. Then Les started walking toward the man. He had a crazy look in his eyes. Now, the Jersey guy kept the cocked gun pointed right at Les, so when Les got close enough the gun pressed right onto his chest. That's when Les reached up slowly and grabbed the barrel and held it to his heart. And all the time he kept screaming, *"Shoot me, shoot me! Come on, shoot me!"*

At this point, everybody was in a state of shock. By now, the Jersey guys had begun to back up. They knew the situation had gotten way out of hand. The man with the gun on Les's chest was beginning to back up now, too, but Les just kept coming with him. The Jersey guys must have been thinking how they would fare in a manslaughter trial in this county with a local jury. Finally, they all broke and ran, including the big shot with the gun on Les. He just dropped his gun and took off. The ridgerunners were too much for them. Les was now standing there holding the barrel of the deer rifle to his chest screaming, "Shoot me!"

We grabbed the deer and dragged it into the woods. Just as we thought, a few rounds were fired into the trees over our heads, so we fired a few rounds back, above the direction where the Jersey guys had gone.

That night, the flatlanders packed up and left their cabin. We all went down to have a beer that night and laugh about how we won our land back. Les was the hero, and all night long one of the boys would stand up, put his finger to his chest like he was holding a gun and say, "Shoot me! Shoot me!"

A few months later, the flatlanders' cabin burned to the ground. The fire chief said it was spontaneous combustion, but everybody knew the spontaneous part was pushing it a bit. Anyway, those Jersey boys got the message, because we have never seen any of them up here again, and every year we hunt right by where their cabin used to stand.

Rifle-Eye Smith
Howard Kisner, Montoursville

This is what Phil Green told me about Rifle-Eye Smith—a man known to everybody up Renovo way a few years back. Rifle-Eye was a Swede, tall and lanky. He worked in the railroad shops up in Westport. He carried an umbrella and a white oak basket wherever he went. He wore a large broad-brimmed black hat. He was a widower and a woman chaser. Some were willing, too, I heard.

They called him Rifle-Eye because his left eye was always squinted like he was sighting with his right eye to shoot out of a gun. When he spoke to you, you'd swear he was taking a bead on you. But that was just his way of looking at the world.

Here's what he done once. He had a nice home down in Westport which he put up for sale. He sold the house for three thousand dollars—a pretty sum, back then. A nice family moved in. After a few months something went wrong. They started seeing strange shapes in the woods. Ghosts and goblins they said came out of the woods at night. They were afraid to be there at night. They asked Rifle-Eye about the ghosts—had they ever bothered him and his family? "Sometimes," he'd say, "especially after the sun went down, but we didn't pay them haunts much mind."

The ghosts got so bad, the wife and kids moved into town. The husband tried everything to get rid of them but failed. Nobody would buy the house. Finally, when the man advertised that he'd take anything for the place, Rifle-Eye came forward and offered him fifteen hundred dollars—just half of what he had sold it for.

The settler eagerly accepted the money. Now Rifle-Eye had bought back his home for half of what he had sold it for.

When folks asked him about the ghosts and how he was doing at night, Rifle-Eye would wink his one good eye, look at them, and say, "Ghosts, I ain't seen hide nor hair of any ghosts."

69

Mose Booney
Clifford Bowersox, Penns Creek

This man is long gone, and what he did is a matter of public record, so I guess it doesn't matter if you write the truth. Mose Booney was a real mountain man who never could fit into the modern world. This was about fifty years ago, down below Middleburg. The story has a bad ending, which you will shortly hear.

Moses Booney came from a family of woodsmen and wanderers. Five brothers and all of them headed west or north or off to war. Mose, as they called him, just headed up into the hills. He was a hunter and was happy to wander the ridges of Jack's or Shade Mountain for days on end. He had camps along the ridges, lean-tos and a cave or two, so it was nothing for him to be gone for days on end.

All the neighbors' dogs barked when Mose walked into town. They wanted to run with him, and often their owners would let them loose because Mose would teach them how to hunt. He was lanky and lean, with a stride long as a spade handle and a handshake hard as hickory slats on the whiskey casks. The man could shoot the eyes out of a horsefly. I've seen him do it. Why, the kids used to gather round him and beg him to do his shooting tricks.

His wife wouldn't let him. Yeah, I know it's strange—him getting married and all. Like a wild thing he just came into rut one fall. He come down with over two hundred pelts, cashed them in, and went to the dance that night with a new suit and a bottle of whiskey. The next morning he was as good as married.

He tried to settle in. He even got a job as a carpenter and worked long days. Sometimes he went logging. Things were all right for a few years. They had two or three kids. Then Mose just couldn't do it any more. He started spending more time in the woods. The old look came back. Mose used nothing but a twenty-two. When the Game Commission said you couldn't use a twenty-two anymore to hunt deer, it made Mose mad. The game wardens were always following Mose, spying on him, and we heard that he shot the tie off one guy just to scare him off. Mose said, "Scare him, hell—I was trying to kill him."

He and his wife lived in a little place right here in the town of Penns Creek. You could always see pelts—bobcat, mink, beaver, muskrat, bear, and deer—hanging out to dry. Trouble was, Mose didn't take kindly to harness. The house, the kids, the mortgage—it was all too much for him. So Mose figured he'd just disappear into the forest and live the life of a mountain man. Not that easy to do when you have a wife and kids.

For months he lived on the lam with the sheriff and deputies tracking him. 'Course, he was a wild thing and they never could touch him. He'd come strolling up to a farmhouse and swap a few pelts for a hot meal and a clean shirt. Then he'd be gone. His sister was in jail, and somehow he got a letter to her

71

that said something like this: "I'm going to turn myself in next Monday morning, but by then it won't make any difference."

When she showed it to the sheriff he said, "What does it mean?"

"Why I think it means he's going to kill himself. That's why it won't make no difference," his sister said.

Well, they thought on it, but by the time Monday came around they still didn't know what to do or where to go, so the sheriff and his men drove on out to the Booney place. And as they approached, they all had a strange feeling, for there hanging from a tree was Mose Booney's red bandanna. They called him, then went inside with guns drawn. There in the kitchen lay Booney's wife with a bullet between her eyes. Beside her, a faint smile on his face, lay the mountain man—dead. He had come home again.

Paddlefoot Khyler
Howard Kisner, Montoursville

Paddlefoot Khyler was a wood hick around the turn of the century up around Renovo and the First Fork of the Sinnemahoning. He had the biggest feet anybody had ever seen. He stood six feet four inches, a great bare-knuckle fighter. In those days, each lumber camp would have its own fighter. The camps would compete and bet on their fighters. It was brutal. No rounds, just knockdowns and a count to see who could continue. They'd fight for hours. The prize money was good.

These fighters had broken their hands so many times that their fists were like huge mallets. You couldn't hurt them.

Well, a lumber camp down in Clearfield along the West Branch of the Suequehanna had a fighter named Reading, and they challenged Khyler to a match. They had the fight around 1900 in Karthus, and the wood hicks come from all over with their walking shoes on. They slung their spiked boots over their shoulders when they had a long way to go.

This Reading man was a big brute. Paddlefoot fought him to a standstill. After an hour, they both lay on the ground and neither one of them could move. The wood hicks wanted to have a rematch, but after that the two men became good friends.

Later on, Paddlefoot became chief of police in Renovo (around World War I). I was ten or eleven at the time this happened. Paddlefoot caught Spits Batchlet robbing a store one night, and they had a big shoot-out. He shot Spits in the head and killed him. I always remembered that years later when I became chief of police in Renovo. I shot at some men to kill them, but they were never close enough for me to hit. I guess I was lucky in that way.

Time passed, the war ended, and Paddlefoot couldn't get around like he used to, so the youngsters started taking advantage of him.

Some teenagers—I was one of them—made a cannon out of the axle from a railroad boxcar. It had about a seven-inch bore and was a few feet long. Back then, you could just go and buy black powder and dynamite and mine squips and blasting caps in the general store.

We got all the stuff we needed, and a few days before the Fourth of July—always a big celebration in the town of Renovo—we started touching our cannon off in the downtown area. *Boom!* Paddlefoot would come a-walking down the street. We'd heft her up and circle around behind him a block or so and touch her off again—*Boom!*

The men of the town got after us, so we moved her up on Breeze Point down from the town and up on a high cliff. We set her off again and again on the Fourth of July. Then we heard they was really after us, so we figured we'd just ditch her and get out of there. Then we did something stupid. We put a big charge of black powder in her and stuffed the ramrod down in and touched her off—*Boom!*

That ramrod shot across the West Branch and ripped into somebody's roof and tore out eight or nine rafters and almost brought the house down. We could hear the crash from where we were.

We toppled the homemade cannon into the river and ran home. Never did get caught, but I always felt Paddlefoot knew who the culprits were all along.

Hoot the Mountain Numbskull
Veris Metzger, Salladasburg

A greenhorn named Adolph Hoot was always getting into trouble up in Salladasburg. One day he was riding his horse along the road when he saw a poor young man on crutches hobbling along the road.

"Excuse me, sir," the young man called to Adolph Hoot. "Can you help me? Some boys have thrown my hat up in a tree?"

Hoot felt sorry for the young man and said, "Of course, I will help you. Where is your hat?"

"It's up in that hemlock tree," said the young man.

So Hoot got off his horse, asked the man to hold the reins, and climbed up in the hemlock tree. He climbed way up, reached out and finally grabbed the hat. "Here's your hat, young man, I've got it," Hoot said.

"That's all right, you can keep it. It's a fair trade we've made for this horse of yours. Thank you," said the young man.

And off he rode and he and the horse were never seen again.

Now, folks began to say Hoot was so green he thought the owls were making fun of him with their "Hoo-hoo-hoot."

"You better cut that out," he would say to the owls. Or sometimes he would blame the hoots on boys he thought were in the bushes.

Because Hoot was always in debt, the sheriff came up from Jersey Shore to get him. Hoot got wind of it and came to our farm, begging my father to hide him. Dad said, "Go in the back room and keep still."

Then the sheriff came and asked if Hoot had been around. While they were talking in the front room, Hoot was banging and bumping into things in the back room. The sheriff knew it had to be Hoot.

"Hoot, come out of there, you darn fool," the sheriff said.

And Hoot, fool that he was, came right out. Last I heard, he got a horse and plow and tried to clear some land to plant crops. He just about killed his horses and himself trying to pull green stumps out of the ground.

Norm Erickson: A Living Legend
Dick Sassaman, Sterling Run

When I was a teenager I liked to hang around Norm Erickson, our former game warden here in Emporium. One November day, I was skinning bear cubs behind his house. The cubs had been shot illegally during the first day of bear season. Back then, you were fined if you shot a cub under a hundred pounds. So the warden and his deputies brought the hides from these bear cubs to the home of the game warden, where they became the property of the Game Commission. So I was working on about three cubs. Well, it was around dusk when this truckload of drunken bear hunters pulled up behind the house, saying they wanted to cut the paws and tail off a couple of the bears Norm had there. See, they were going to go to the bars and brag about the paws as if they had killed the bears themselves.

They knocked on the back door and asked Fran, Norm's wife, if they could cut a few paws off. She said no, definitely not, but after she went back inside, a couple of them came over to where I was and cut four paws off. Then they took off.

About an hour later, Norm came home. When he heard the news, he was steamed. He was mad at me for letting it happen. He had a savage look when I heard him say, "I know where they are. I'll find these guys."

So Norm drove from bar to bar until he found the car Fran had described to him. He went into the bar and saw three guys passing those little paws around. It made him so mad he pulled them all outside where he fined them each two hundred dollars for removing parts of a bear that had been killed illegally. So their little escapade cost them six hundred dollars. That was Norm. If he wanted to get you, he'd find a way.

Another time, a fellow from downstate pulled in a private farm road beside a field, parked his car, and went down to Dents Run to go fishing. Pretty soon afterwards, a young farm boy drives up in a tractor with a spreader just loaded with manure. The fisherman's car blocks the road, so the young man can't haul the manure to the field. After trying to maneuver around the car, the teenager gets angry. He turns tractor and spreader around and just unloads the manure all over the man's white car. Then the boy drives away.

By the time the fisherman returns, the acid from the manure has eaten through the vinyl on the hood of the car, leaving nasty scars. The fisherman sees his car and goes nuts. He's ready to kill. Somehow he manages to get the car into town with the windshield wipers pushing the stuff from side to side, and he finds a place to wash the manure off. People

77

laugh and point at the manure-covered car. Kids can smell it a mile away. Humiliated, the man drives back downstate, talks to his lawyer, talks to his insurance agent, the police. They suggest he give it up and just forget it. He doesn't. A week later he returns to Emporium, goes to the police, the Department of Forestry, and finally the game warden, Norm Erickson. Norm listens with great sympathy. The man feels he finally has found someone who will arrest the kid, put him behind bars, send him away for life.

Norm looks at the man long and shakes his head. He sighs. Then he whips out his pad and writes the man up for a thirty-dollar fine for blocking a public road.

Prince Farrington and the Mayor
Warren Searfoss, South Williamsport

Prince Farrington came from the Carolinas and he started into farming up on a ridge around Loganton over in Sugar Valley. He honestly believed that a man should have the right to make his own good whiskey, and by golly he could make good whiskey. It was white, corn whiskey. He didn't put any coloring in.

As time went by, he taught other people in the hills to make it as good as he did and then Prohibition came. He started selling the "white mule" whiskey and he made a fortune.

I worked for the Ralston Company, and I sold feed

to the farmers all over central Pennsylvania. Soon
Prince bought farms in Antes Fort and Jersey Shore
with the money he made. He raised dairy cows, beef
cows, chickens, hogs, and silver foxes on his farm.
He hired lots of people and helped lots of people
out. Sometimes he'd pay off people's mortgages or
actually give them money when they were in need.
There's not an unkind word anyone along the West
Branch can say about Prince Farrington.

One day in 1931 I drove out to the house in
Antes Fort. It still stands—the one right after the
second bridge over the river. Big white house on the
right. I drove out to get his feed order. I was shocked
to see Prince talking to two policemen. One was a
state policeman and one was a Williamsport
policeman. And there in the barn, ready for
shipment, were kegs of whiskey stacked up to the
roof. After they left, I said to him "Prince, how can
you leave this stuff here with the police snooping
around?"

He just shrugged and said, "Oh I'm just arranging
to have a truckload of whiskey shipped into New
York State. Those guys are arranging a safe trip out
of Williamsport and on up Route 15. I pay them off.
But they're so greedy. They keep demanding more
and more payoffs. It makes me kind of sick to see
these so-called honorable law enforcement officers so
greedy."

Now, Prince was pretty safe during Prohibition
because even the most "honorable" of the politicians
and policemen and FBI people were in on the take.
In fact, one guy who protected Prince—for money,
of course—later turned against him. He prosecuted

the Prince after Prohibition to make a name for himself. And I think Prince had to flee down south, though I'm told they brought him back in rags and he died. He did do some time, though, at Lewisburg Prison. The prison is near Bucknell University, and the Prince said he was "going to college."

Anyway, this former FBI man later became a fine upstanding citizen. He even became the mayor of State College. His past was all left behind him. Years later, something odd happened. I was back at Penn State for a reunion. One of my fraternity brothers had too much to drink, and another brother and I were escorting him down the street to where we were staying. We were passing the town hall when I saw the mayor come out on the steps with two policemen. (I later heard he was cracking down on public drunkenness.) He pointed down at us, and the policemen came on down to arrest my friend. I looked both of them in the eyes and said, "I want you to go back and tell your mayor that if he arrests my friend here I will go to the newspapers and make public his connections with bootlegging in the 1930s."

One of the policemen walked back up to the mayor and delivered my message. Then the mayor waved his hand as if to say, "Let him go," and he quickly turned and walked into City Hall.

Yes, it is true that during Prohibition nearly everybody broke the law, but some on the side of the law were out-and-out crooks, and some of the moonshiners were, like Prince Farrington, the kindest people you'd ever know. Prince was a Robin Hood of the Depression years, that's for sure.

The Prince and the Doctor
George Porter, Jersey Shore

I remember when they had a big whiskey raid over
on the Bland at Prince Farrington's place back in
the early thirties. The feds came in and broke up
many oak barrels of whiskey. Word went out and
men came from miles around to watch. Now, there
was so much whiskey running on the ground that it
began to pool up. You see, it was the dead of winter
and the puddles were frozen in the ruts. Well, the
man came, and after the cops and feds left they
began to scoop up the whiskey and to drink it and
have a party outdoors. That's how good Prince
Farrington's whiskey was. You didn't want to waste a
drop.

And I'll tell you some more about Prince's
whiskey. My grandfather was Dr. Tullius over in
Beech Creek. Now, there was quite a guy. Yes, there
is a strong family resemblance, and I thank you,
because that's quite a compliment. He had the first
cars in Beech Creek. He punched out a German
barber before the First War for talking up Germany.
And folks came from all over Beech Creek and put
American flags in his barber shop and told him to
leave them there.

Dr. Tullius owned the bank in town. One day
three armed robbers hit the bank and made off with
thousands of dollars. Dr. Tullius gave chase and shot
one of the robbers and helped capture the other two.
He was a brave man. Now, Gladys Porter, who is my
wife and Prince Farrington's daughter, tells of how

81

her father would take the kids all the way to Beech Creek to get their vaccinations. "That's a long way from Jersey Shore to get shots," she used to say to Prince. But he was going to supply the doc with whiskey. Of course, doctors need whiskey for medicinal purposes, but they also needed it for personal purposes, and Dr. Tullius was no exception.

The Prince and the Feds
Lester Pfirman, Nesbit, and Billy Wolfe, Slate Run

Most of the old-timers went to school right here in this schoolhouse. We lived over in the Nippenose Valley. Now those kids go to Jersey Shore High School. Here, look at these old pictures of Nippono Park. It's all gone now, but back then it was our swimming pool, yacht club, and skating pond. The West Branch of the Susquehanna.

Those of us who are over seventy years old saw the park change. It was there in the days of logging and in the days of the railroad. Trains would roll through all day long while we were swimming in the summer or ice skating in winter. We could hop a freight to go to Jersey Shore.

Prince Farrington? We don't talk much about him today; he was the biggest thing around these parts, though, in his day. He was the kindest man in the county. Give you the shirt off his back, and they put him in jail just for making good whiskey. Even when they would confiscate the hooch, it had the habit of evaporating. The stone house they call the Gap Country Store, right there in the gap, is where the Prince used to store his whiskey casks. He had people cooking for him all over these valleys.

He had a hog farm right down there across the valley, down on Dead Man's Turn. He'd make the whiskey and feed the mash to the hogs. A real neat operation. Prince also had a farm up at Corbett Deadwater on Pine Creek, and he'd stash whiskey there, too. He got warned when the revenuers were coming. They would roll the casks out of the barn and tie them under water in Pine Creek. Tie them to railroad ties on the bottom. The federals would find nothing. Then Prince would send two boys out with knives to cut the casks loose. Funny it was to see them come bobbing up in Pine Creek. Mark Dunkel was one of those kids. He said Prince had false gas tanks put on his trucks to haul whiskey.

Like we said, we don't talk much about Prince anymore. Too many memories.

4

SNAKEBITE
Disasters and Hard Times

P EOPLE IN THIS CHAPTER TELL stories about disaster, danger, and death. All these stories are true, I am told, and many are narrated by the people who actually lived through the ordeals or witnessed the events firsthand. When people tell disaster tales, they often get animated and intensely involved— more than for other kinds of stories. Indeed, tragedy, dangerous action, and fear bring out the best in Pennsylvania storytellers.

Disasters cover the front pages of our newspapers and our television screens. We read and watch because these events are so extraordinary that they grab our attention. Moreover, they are not only sensational and horrible—they also did not happen to us. We can watch in safety. A battle might be fascinating to watch from a distance, but up close, in the line of fire, a battle is terrifying. Even a person who experienced peril firsthand can, when danger passes, enjoy telling a story about it. So when Dick Sassaman, one of our storytellers, describes the scanner waking him up at night to report a plane crash in the mountains, the story gives us the thrill without the risk, and that gives us satisfaction.

Norm Erickson, the retired game protector of Emporium, told me the "Snakebite" story in his backyard one summer day. He held out a discolored hand and showed me the bluish blotches on his arm marked over forty years ago by the fangs of two timber rattlers. He described his ordeal in great detail. The meaning of Erickson's tale is survival, coming back after a horrible accident. His story forms part of a legend: the tough woodsman humbled by nature who springs back into action nevertheless. "Shocked," about an accidental encounter with a high-voltage cable, again comes from Erickson.

Doc Dornish, the retired postmaster of St. Marys, told me about the great influenza epidemic of 1918, when more Americans succumbed to the disease than died in World War I. Spreading over the country in a few weeks' time, the deadly virus caused a panic. Many people, especially the elderly who were most vulnerable, shunned all contact with people, and some would not allow even family members to come near them.

I collected "Miracle Cure" from four firsthand sources, including the parents of the sick child and the healer. All agree that he was better after the healing ceremony. I have talked with the boy and watched him work; despite his handicaps he does remarkably well.

"Turkey Hunting Accidents" were told by Gene Fessler of Covington, and the boy involved is Ted Kelchner. "Mom's Dying" comes from Kim Winter, who left the area after her husband's death. She loved the country, but the rough rural people sometimes frightened her. She told her story with a certain distaste.

"Prospecting in Alaska" was told by an engineer working for the Army Corps of Engineers on the Cowanesque Dam. I met him while helping Dan Usavage of Wellsboro move a stove or piano into his house. After the job was over, he told his story. Robert Lyon's tale, "Death in the Blizzard," testifies to the hard times in rural Pennsylvania in the first thirty years of the century. His story has the ring of authenticity.

The bizarre anonymous story, "Accidental Fire," illustrates how even decisions by the state police can reflect rural values: insiders close up ranks and keep the community's secrets. Dick Sassaman, the forestry technician of Sterling Run, describes two rescues. He has been on scores of rescues and knows the hazards, the odds. His story of Amish men on a youthful spree has a ludicrous side; on the other hand, the airplane wreck he witnessed, described in "Two Rescue Missions," is the real thing.

Snakebite
Norm Erickson, Emporium

I fought with General Patton in the Battle of the Bulge, but the closest I ever came to death was on May 19, 1949, when I was working as a game warden. My deputy and I were up on Whippoorwill Run checking out the hollows, and we were on foot. We had left the car, a Model A, three miles away at Bigger Run. We were walking through a stony field and it was hot. Suddenly I tripped and fell face-down into a hollow in the rocks. I put out both hands to ease the fall, and as they hit the ground I felt a hot stinging in my hand and arm. Then I saw them—two brown rattlers caked with mud, fresh out of hibernation, their fangs sunk into the flesh of my right hand.

I screamed and rolled away, shaking one off, but

the other rattler's fangs had gone deep to the bone.
I tore that one off with my left hand, leaving two
long gashes in my third finger. By now, my friend
was with me. We both knew it was going to be
bad. You see, when you see people handling
rattlesnakes at these snakehunt festivals, those
snakes have already spit out most of their venom. If
you get bit then, it's not so bad. But to get bit by a
snake in the deep woods that nobody has bothered
or handled—well, you're talking about a different
kind of snakebite. Now, I had taken two of those
hits. We had three miles to go to get to the car.
My friend almost carried me some of the way. The
first mile my arm began to swell. We stopped and
cut my fingers to let some of the poisoned blood
out. By the second mile I was getting dizzy, and
by the third mile I was getting worse and worse.
There is no pain like rattlesnake vemon in your
system.

Well, my friend loaded me in the car and drove to
the hospital. On the way he said, "If the pain gets
any worse, I can always shoot you, Norm."

Somehow that wisecrack kept me going. Truth is,
I should have died. The venom crawled up my veins,
wrapped around my heart, and tried to squeeze me to
death. I went into shock, I ran a high fever; my arm
and then my whole right side swelled up like a giant
sausage. I lay there semiconscious for a week in St.
Marys Hospital. It was worse when I came out of it
because the pain was greater. Now my right side and
my arm had great clusters of blue and purple veins
swollen like grapes. Food would make me sick. I lost
forty-five pounds.

89

During all this time I was a sort of freak. I was in the corner of a big ward in the hospital and thirty or forty curious people would come to see me every day. Not that many people get snakebit; folks wanted to see just how bad it really was. It was bad enough for me. It was eight months before I could walk right, and to this day I still can't use my right hand very well. You can see how blue the fingers and the inside of my arm still are. That's almost forty years ago.

I'm sort of famous for getting snakebit. Fact is, I was bitten again by a rattler about twelve years later. I was bending down to get a key out of a wooden box so I could open a gate to the game lands when I saw it coming at my hand. Once bitten, twice shy. I dreaded getting bitten so much, yet here it was all over again like I was fated to get bitten. These thoughts ran through my mind as I saw the white fangs closing in on my hand. It seemed to take forever for the snake to sink its fangs into my left hand.

I shook it off quickly and ran for the Scout. At least this time I'd get out fast, and I'd go to another hospital—to Coudersport. As I drove down the mountain, the blood was spurting out of my hand onto the windshield. I didn't notice it till later when my wife was driving me to the hospital. This time I knew what to expect. They had some antidote but it didn't do much good. The same swelling, the same agony. I almost died again. In fact, this time the pain was worse—maybe because I was older, but of course it didn't kill me.

90

Shocked
Norm Erickson, Emporium

I'm a game warden and game wardens are supposed
to have a suspicious nature. That's why when I
saw the dead deer under the power line at the head
of Dent's Run I was sure those teenage boys were up
to their old tricks again. I had been cruising the state
game lands in Cameron County, and I stopped to
look down the valley. I noticed one of the high-
tension wires was hanging low near where the deer
lay, but I didn't give it any thought as I climbed
down the hill. I was so mad at those kids I could
hardly think straight.

I came down on the side of the wire where the
deer was and I examined the animal. No sign of a
bullet anywhere. I looked around. I walked over
toward the electric wire, and I ducked under it.
Then it happened; the juice hit me and sent me into
the woods sprawling. I thought I had been shot by a
gun, and I thought I was dying or already dead.

When I came to, I realized what had happened—
I had brushed the power line. The winter storms
had lowered it. I struggled to my feet and managed
to crawl up the hill and get in the Scout. Then
I drove slowly back into Emporium. I walked into
the state police station to report the low power
line. I must have been in a daze. I had no idea
what I looked like. A bunch of the troopers came
up to me and said, "my God, what happened
to you?"

91

Then they showed me what I looked like. My shoes were all singed. The metal eyelets had burned holes into my skin. My hair was partly burned and I had a burn down my back where my shirt was ripped. Why I lived is a mystery to me. It was a mystery to the doctor, too. Thousands of volts of current had hit me and somehow I had lived.

Influenza
Doc Dornish, St. Marys

The influenza epidemic hit St. Marys during the First World War. Winter it was, and people were dying. The young ones seemed to get over it, but the old died. My one grandmother lived alone down by the pond. She convinced herself that the flu would kill her, so she kept everybody away from her house that winter.

I was a teenager and I had just got a new twenty-gauge shotgun. I went down to the pond to try to shoot some shore birds. We called them snipe. It was a freezing cold January day. While walking across a frozen cove, I fell through the ice. It was only about three feet deep. The shock was awful. With my gun, I ran to my grandmother's house. I knew she would let me in.

I pounded in the door. It was locked, of course. Then I saw her face. It had a look of fear on it. She never saw my frozen clothes—all she saw was a boy who might be carrying influenza. "Go down the road to Nanny's," she said. Nanny was my other grandmother. I couldn't believe it. By then I was shivering so bad I could hardly run, but I made it to Nanny's. Without a word, she stripped my clothes off, poured two shots of whiskey down my throat, and dragged me off to the tub were she parboiled me for two hours. The fact that she had to see me naked didn't bother her—she did what she had to do. That's the way people were in those days. After that, I became more aware of the flu, of just how many people were dying.

We had a place in town called the Tenbro. The hired hands and railroad men without families stayed there. Many of them died. A certain doctor would walk in there to check out the men. He would just give them a brief glance and then charge them forty dollars. Another man in town made and sold a lot of patent medicine during the epidemic. It was mostly whiskey, but folks said it seemed to help. That was a bad time in St. Marys.

Miracle Cure
Harry, Mary, Wes, and Sara, Lycoming County

Today my boy can walk almost normal and can work in the shop with my husband. But three years ago he could do almost nothing because of his terrible seizures. We had to watch him constantly, make him wear a helmet, and make him take all kinds of drugs. That was before the folks in that Williamsport church performed the miracle cure.

Some young married couples started a church downtown. They wanted a church where they could really show it when the spirit moved them. My husband heard about it and we both decided to go. Pentecostals they were. They would do the laying-on of hands and the speaking in tongues. Oh, my husband liked that kind of thing. One time I felt the Spirit come over me and I dropped to the floor and started shouting for joy. What a wonderful feeling!

Now, we never took our boy to church because of his problems, but one day three of the members were out at our farm and met him. I remember one of the men was very shy. After talking to our son for a long time, he came over to us and said, "I believe I can cure that boy."

Well, this got something started. The entire congregation got mighty curious about what was happening. See, they were beginning to believe the Lord was working through that shy man. Everyone decided to hold a special service for the healing of my son. At the end of the service, the man would step forward and attempt to heal my son with the prayerful help of the congregation.

When the special day came, we dressed up our boy and drove into Williamsport. He seemed to know exactly what was going on, and he was happier and calmer than I have ever seen him. As we led him inside the packed church, I could hear gasps from some of the people who had never seen him. With his legs twisted and the helmet on his head, he could barely walk with the aid of a cane and his parents holding him up. He looked so hopeless I could tell right then that some had lost faith in the power of the shy man to heal him. But my boy just smiled sweetly and looked up at the altar.

After the service, the prayers, and the singing, the time for healing came. Two strong men carried my boy up onto the altar while the shy man walked up behind them. Then he stood above my son and turned to face the congregation. When he raised his arms, the sleeves of his robe looked like angel wings, and a ray of sunlight landed on his face. He laid his hands on my son, looked up, and began a loud prayer. "Oh, heavenly Father, give this young man health that he may prosper. Take away his limp, his epilepsy, his fevers. We ask you, Oh Lord, to heal this man. Heal, heal, heal," he kept saying.

Finally, he was screaming it out, and my boy was screaming, and we all were screaming, "Heal, heal, heal!"

And you could feel the power grow until it got to be too much, and then they fell backwards on the altar.

Then it was real quiet. The first thing I noticed when the boy came to were his eyes—they were clear, focused. He looked around like he was coming out of a dream and said, "Where am I?"

That was two years ago. Right after the cure, he began to walk, his seizures went down to almost nothing, and he began working in the garden. My boy became a different person. As far as I can tell, it was a true miracle cure. That's what everybody in the church said too. A true miracle cure.

Turkey Hunting Accidents
Gene Fessler, Covington

Every year a fair number of us Pennsylvania hunters get ourselves shot and even killed by other hunters. The madness of deer season must be the most dangerous time, with bullets clipping trees over our heads and kids scoping us out with loaded rifles. Still, most of us fear turkey season more. We expect stray bullets flying in deer season, but in turkey season the hunter often feels more like the one hunted. In spring gobbler season, camouflaged hunters calling in lovesick birds often lure in other hunters instead. In fall season, nervous woodsmen prowl the forest with high-powered rifles just itching to spot the hard-to-find birds. They begin to see birds that aren't there. And that's when someone is liable to—as we say—"get shot for a turkey."

Last year, two guys from Altoona were turkey hunting high up on a ridge. All morning they pushed along, then stopped to rest about sixty yards apart. One sat up on the ridge while the other stopped below in a laurel thicket. The hunter on the ridge noticed another hunter out ahead of him on the same ridge. As he watched the other hunter, he noticed the man was raising his gun, looking below, using his scope to sight in on something. Suddenly he realized the hunter was sighting in on his friend, thinking he was a turkey. Just as he screamed at him the hunter shot.

After the shot, the woods got quiet. He knew his buddy had been hit, so he kept on yelling until the hunter heard him. The man who had just shot his friend turned and looked at him. For a moment he thought the hunter would shoot him, too—for what he had seen. Then they both turned and looked downhill toward the man who had been shot.

They got to him at about the same time.

"Christ, I thought he was a turkey, for sure," the stranger said.

The wounded man was lying there with a hole in his shoulder bleeding dark and fast. The man who shot him did something then that the doctors said saved his life. He took off the wounded man's suspenders made a bandage over the wound, and then wrapped it up tight and tied it off with the braces. Then they started to carry him out because they both knew if they went for help he would bleed to death.

Now, a mountain rescue is one kind of thing, but lugging a grown man out of the woods is another. They carried and dragged and bounced and rolled him for nearly three miles. By the time they got him to a forest road, his buddy was mad at him for getting himself shot.

No charges were filed against the hunter for shooting the man. The wounded man's buddy told police that the shooting was just a misunderstanding, and that the hunter was a great help in getting his friend out of the woods alive. In fact, he said the hunter probably saved his friend's life after shooting him, and his friend was sort of acting like a turkey down there anyway.

The man who was shot for a turkey recovered and now leads a normal life, but the friend who helped drag him out doesn't even talk to him, and neither of them go hunting any more.

Did I tell you about the guy who made turkey calls out of metal and pieces of balloon? They fit right in his mouth. He was the best turkey caller in Tioga County, but he doesn't hunt at all after what happened to him two years ago. He was hunting up in Covington and one of his calls got stuck back in his throat. He could breathe, but having this thing stuck in his throat made him panicky, so he ran down to the motel and staggered up to the bar.

"I thought he was speaking Spanish," Earlene said, recalling his first attempt to talk.

"I thought he was taking a fit," Billy said.

Finally somebody figured out what was wrong and called an ambulance. A few days later, all his friends brought a present to him in the hospital—a mouth call like the one he swallowed, only this one was six feet long.

Another turkey-hunting accident took place this fall on the state game lands near Arnot. After hunting too late, a father and his teenage son were hustling to get out of the woods while they could still see. Suddenly the boy slipped and his shotgun went off, hitting his father in the leg. Of course, the gun shouldn't have been loaded and they shouldn't have been jogging along like they were. Anyway, the father tells the boy to keep on going, to try to get to the road and get some help.

The boy finally did cut a road and ran on down to a farmhouse and they got the ambulance and rescue squad up there. By then it was dark and the boy had no idea where he left his father. So, grabbing their lights, the rescue teams split up and started into the woods. It looked like they would be at it for a long time. An hour later and a mile into the woods, a sixteen-year-old named Teddy Kelchner found the man lying on the ground shivering and bleeding. His left thigh looked like hamburger. Teddy knew the man had gone into shock, so immediately he stripped down to just his underpants and boots and wrapped the man in his own clothes.

Then he found the man's gun and fired a few rounds into the air to tell the others he had found the man. But he knew the echoes from the shots would only confuse the rescuers. They wouldn't know where he was. So Teddy asked the man if he had a whistle and the man moaned and pointed to his pocket. You see, even though they were running out of the woods with loaded guns at dark, they had taken the precaution of carrying whistles in case one of them got lost. So Teddy started blowing the whistle at regular intervals and pretty soon the rescuers found them and carried the man out of the woods on a stretcher with an IV in his arm. He healed up fine, too. His son who shot him went on to college and Teddy did too. Yessir, he's a smart one, saved that man's life.

Mom's Dying
Kim Winter, Elk Grove

This took place up on North Mountain back in the nineteen sixties. My husband George was

retired then, and we settled on a farm above Elk
Grove and raised beef cattle. That's a nice kind of
gentleman farming for a retired banker, and the tax
breaks are good too. Well, up on the mountain lived
some rough ridgerunner kind of families. We didn't
know them at all, but we saw them go by and they
were poor. I understand some of the children didn't
even go to school.

One day while George was in Bloomsburg, I heard
a knock at the back door. There stood a girl about
eleven years old. She had stringy brown hair, dirty
hands, face and legs, and a grubby print dress. She
was wearing boys' high-top sneakers way too big for
her. "Yes," I said, "What can I do for you, my
child?"

"Mom's dyin'," was all she said. And she looked
up at me with big brown eyes and pointed up toward
North Mountain. I brought her inside and tried to
get her to tell me more, but all she'd say was,
"Mom's dying." Finally, George came home and I
made him try to drive us up the mountain in the
Scout. The little girl took us up some of the God-
awfullest paths I ever saw. They seemed more like
deer paths than roads, but George managed to buck
and lurch us up on top of the ridge to a shack built
onto an old trailer.

"My God," George said, "I didn't know anybody
lived up here. I heard there were some pretty mean
men up in the woods, but I didn't know they had
families and lived this far off the road."

The girl took us inside. She seemed careful, almost
scared, because she looked around. She led us into
the shack which was all one room. There on a couch

lay the mother looking dead; beside her sat a younger girl just staring at us.

"Jesus," said George. "we better get her out of here."

I went over and felt her pulse. She was still alive, but her pulse was slow. It seemed like she was in a trance. We carried her out to the car and took the two kids along to the hospital. When we got there the nurse asked her last name. "Diller," the little girl said.

The nurse looked at George and at me. "Does Mr. Diller know you're here?" she said.

"No, we're just neighbors, helping out in an emergency," George said. "We don't even know these people."

"Oh, I see," the nurse said. "Well, Mrs. Diller has had these spells before. Seems to be some sort of a seizure brought on by stress, often when her husband roughs her up. We've been through this before. She pulls out of it in a day or two. Then she goes home. We've been trying to get her and the kids into a shelter or some low-income housing in town, but you know how it is with these mountain people. They just want to live in the hills. But I want to warn you about Mr. Diller."

"What about him?" George said.

The nurse turned to leave. She looked back over her shoulder and said, "He doesn't like outsiders, especially when they meddle in his family affairs. You better leave the kids right here. He'll be down to collect them sometime soon. It would be a mistake to take them home."

So we went on home and put the incident out of

our minds. Then one afternoon I stopped in a little grocery store and the young woman who waited on me looked me in the eye and said, "You best watch out for Mr. Diller. I think he's going to get your husband for snatching his wife and kids."

After that, George stayed home. He carried a pistol when he left the house, and we locked the doors all the time. Then one afternoon George was out in the fields mowing hay, and he looked up and saw a tall haggard man come staggering out of the woods with a hatchet in his hand. As he came forward, George pulled his gun and pulled off the safety. The man—and it *was* Mr. Diller, George found out later—stopped a few yards away from the tractor and put up his hand. "Don't shoot, mister. I ain't after you any more," the man said. "It's my son I'm after. If I catch him I'll kill him. Which way did he go?"

After that, George stopped worrying about Mr. Diller. Fact is, I think they put Diller under some kind of observation or something. He never did anything really wrong, but he sure wasn't right.

That's not the end of the story, though. A few months later, when everything had got back to normal, I was making pies in the kitchen one afternoon when I heard a quiet knock on the back door. I went to the door and who did I see but the little Diller girl in the same dress and sneakers. "What is it, child?" I said.

She looked at me with those brown eyes and said, "Mom's dying."

Accidental Fire
A State Trooper's Wife

I know about this because my husband is a state trooper and I get the inside scoop. Only I'm not supposed to tell, but anyhow here's the story. The night that Nobby Wilkerson's house burned to the ground was the last time anybody saw Dud Smith alive. Nobby and Dud were neighbors, separated by a hill and two fields. Dud's wife, Helen, called the police later on the night of the fire to report Dud missing. Nobody made any connection between the fire and Dud's disappearance until a few days later.

Little Jimmie Tice was cutting across the field two days later and found Dud face down in the grass. The coroner said Dud had been dead "for some time." Ever wonder how long that is? In Dud's pockets the police found four large, empty cans of lighter fluid. Cause of death was a heart attack. Later on, my husband told me the time of death was Monday night—the same time as Nobby's fire. But why would Dud burn his neighbor's house down?

Some of us knew. Dud's wife Helen and Nobby had been having an affair for the past three years. They had broken it off for a while—largely because of Dud's bad heart condition. Nobby even moved to another town, but after a year away he moved back and started up again with Helen. It must have been too much for Dud. So he had taken his revenge. At least, that was the opinion of everyone in the valley, and that was everyone who mattered or cared.

Now, the state troopers faced a problem: should they

charge a dead man with arson and let everybody in on the motive behind Dud's action? Or should they just say it was an accident with Dud's death nearby just a coincidence? Already Joe Thomas, the fire chief, was calling it arson and pointing a finger at the dead man. But Joe disliked Dud because when Dud worked for the borough he would never leave cinders on Joe's hill after a heavy snow. The troopers knew everything, but they couldn't see raking up the past and hurting Helen and Nobby and Dud's memory. But they had to explain in their reports what happened so it made sense, and they had to give a reason for everything that night. They had the final say in the investigation. This is what they finally decided to put in the report:

Nobby's Wilkerson's fire was accidental. Dud Smith died of a heart attack brought on by unusual circumstances: a heavy smoker with a bad heart, he carried tins of lighter to ensure his lighters would work. The night of Nobby's fire Dud was walking the hill between the two houses for his daily exercise. The air was thick with smoke, making breathing hard for Dud as he walked uphill, so hard it triggered a fatal heart attack.

So that's the way they wrote it all up, and that's the way it officially happened. Let sleeping dogs lie.

Two Rescue Missions
Dick Sassaman, Sterling Run

I work on the Emporium Search and Rescue Squad. Our busiest time of year is the fall hunting season.

With so many wooded areas in Cameron, Clinton, and Elk counties, and so many hunters in the woods, people are bound to get lost. We got a call by CB from deep in the woods: the neighboring cabin had a problem. When we got there, we found a cabin filled with twenty young Amish men. Piles of cigarette butts and maybe a couple of bottles of applejack littered the dining room table. Amish have a tradition that lets young men raise hell before they become official members of the church. These guys were making the most of it.

Probably they had gone hunting before the season opened. They said they were just looking, but they had their rifles just in case. Well, Brother Irving got separated from the rest of the flock somewhere up in the hollow, and they hadn't seen him for five hours. By this time it was one o'clock in the morning.

The rescue team included a policeman with bloodhounds. They could track down anything. He could speak good Dutch, too, so the Amish told him the truth about everything.

We worked back and forth up a big hollow until our batteries went out; we changed them and again they went out. We had one flashlight left. We tracked Irving for about six miles, and finally we heard three shots up above us. Soon there comes Irving bouncing down the hill, waving and carrying his rifle, which got him into trouble in the first place. Instead of Amish shoes he had on fancy, cowboy boots with high heels.

No sooner did we settle him down and start back to their cabin than he reaches in his wallet, takes out a big wad of bills, and starts trying to pay us. We just laughed. When we arrived back at camp, three of the older boys took old Irving in a back room and began to yell at him. My friend the policeman could understand and he said they were really scolding him.

Another rescue call I remember ended in tragedy. Late one winter night I awoke when I heard the scanner tell the police to drive up Whittimore Mountain, look to the west, and see if they could see fire. I knew right away a plane was down. I didn't go in with the first team. They took the jeeps in as far as they could go and then switched to snowmobiles. The planes making for St. Mary's airport have mountains in their way, and if they get careless they can clip the trees. That's what this plane did. The two men were flying in to pick up important machinery from a factory in St. Marys.

I went in second day: of course, there was no rescue, no salvage, just two cremated corpses. We put the remains of each man in a body bag, and folded the bag over three times. Nothing much there. Loaded with fuel, the plane just exploded as it cut a swath through the trees. You could see where the titanium propeller tore apart as it cut into the trees. You expect that in airplane crashes.

Death in the Blizzard
Robert Lyon, St. Mary

For pure tragedy and hard times, this is about the worst I ever heard. Back in the 1920s, the state used to run these big preserves where hunting was forbidden. A man with a wife and young son was hired by the Game Commission to live on the preserve deep in the woods of Cameron County. The man would tend the preserve by keeping poachers off and making sure the animals were thriving. Of course, those preserves are long gone.

The story begins in January during a terrible blizzard. The storm stranded everybody in northern Pennsylvania; even if you had a sled, you couldn't go far. Now, the family out on the preserve had weathered out blizzards before, so the storm didn't mean much to them. The woman was pregnant and due any time, but that didn't worry them because she had managed before. During the height of the storm, the man and the boy went down to the creek to draw some water. While they were hauling out the water, the boy suddenly slipped, falling into the moving water, and was washed down under the frozen part of the creek. Frantic, the father ran along the creek trying to break through the ice. Finally, he was able to break through and pull the boy out.

When the father saw the boy wasn't breathing, he panicked. If only he could get the boy to the hospital in Emporium he would be all right. They would bring him around. Perhaps the boy was already dead or perhaps he could have revived him—we will never know. But the howling blizzard and the horror of it all made the man and his wife a little crazy. All they could think of was getting him to a hospital. So they piled blankets on the boy and put him in the Model A Ford and cranked up the car and tried to drive the fifteen miles to Emporium.

They didn't plow roads back then. How he ever

got the car out of the preserve no one ever knew. Later on, he said he had to get out and shovel fifteen times. Out on the road to Emporium they hit four-foot drifts, but somehow they managed to keep on toward town. By now the boy had turned blue in his mother's arms, but she didn't notice his color or how cold he was. A few miles out of Emporium they stuck in a big drift. Then the man decided to run on into town for help. The woman stayed in the car cradling her dead son in her arms.

Then it started so snow again, hard. Now in their panic to save the boy, the mother and father had forgotten about the unborn child the mother was carrying. As she sat there holding her son, the baby began to stir within her, and soon the child was on its way. She had to let go of her dead boy and make room for the new child coming out in the midst of the howling storm.

When the rescue party came two hours later, they saw something amazing: a woman holding a newborn baby girl in her arms, and, sitting next to her, the corpse of her older child had turned blue and rigid as if it was the blizzard making him cold and not death. The rescuers could long remember the howls of the blizzard mixing with the cries of the newborn baby.

My uncle was on the rescue squad and he told me all about it. That baby girl is an old woman today with sixteen grandchildren. She could tell this story better than me because it's her story. You can't hardly get stories that good any more.

5

THE SHERIFF'S WIFE
True Stories

EXTENDED NARRATIVES OF TRUE
events, often raised to an artistic level,
characterize the Pennsylvania storyteller's
most reliable art form. Everyone loves to
take something that really happened, dress it up, and
tell it on a special occasion. In fact, it is considered
a necessary social grace in many communities and
business circles. What good is a salesperson who
can't tell a story, or a teacher, or a coach, or a
parent? Coaches, in fact, seem to all go to the same
school to learn how to tell true stories, and most of
them are very good at it.

These stories are also part of a storyteller's repertoire;
they have been told before and will be told again. Each
is a performance, not a one-time telling. While the
folktale takes us out of everyday experience—
we expect fantastic and miraculous events,
transformations, and sudden changes in individuals—
in the extended anecdote or true story the realm isn't
magical, it is everyday reality, but a heightened or
intensified version of it. A true story can simply amuse,
but more often it reinforces community values and
unconsciously shapes those values. They must have a
point, and they must also illustrate or shore up an often
unarticulated belief. We expect certain values to be
put to the test in these stories.

For this reason, these stories are seldom told to
outsiders. Listeners have to be part of a group that
shares the values embedded within the story. So the
telling and the listening serve also as a form of
community bonding. Each story touches on an
important value held by the community. An example
is "The Sheriff's Wife," told to me by a woman

schoolteacher. (I have changed the story somewhat.) It clearly condemns the man, pities the woman, and defends the family.

A story may serve as a safety valve for the release of tension. "Praise the Lord and Fill the Tank" comes from Professor Larry Miller of Wellsboro, who ran a county mental health clinic before going into teaching. Stories like this must have relieved the strain of his work. It comes close to disaster but always slips back into the comic. An outrageous interruption of a solemn church service fulfills a classic comic formula. "Flying Baby Jesus," told by Michael Martin of Roaring Spring, is pure slapstick.

A number of stories touch humorously on breaking the law. "Shotlight" comes from Dick Sassaman of Sterling Run. "Beer Robbery" recounts the hijinks of college boys who have long since straightened out, but still recall their drunken escapade with sheepish amusement.

As can be seen in Dick Sassaman's tale, "Deputy Fish Warden," lawmen themselves are often the objects of criticism or ridicule. Norm Erickson of Emporium tells "The State Trooper and the Turkey" and "Frosty the Poacher." Compared to Frosty, who is willing to take his medicine when he gets caught, the poaching done by the policeman looks even more criminal. "Liquor Control Board," by Howard Kistner, a retired lawman of Montoursville, describes a rookie state trooper's realization of the corruption to be found at all levels of state government. Or was no one immune from lawbreaking during Prohibition?

"The Great Flood" describes the disastrous result of Hurricane Agnes, which struck the Northeast in

1972. Both Benny Tacka and Dave Darby of Blossburg, excellent storytellers, gave me versions of the flood. While I was at the very spot where this story takes place, as a volunteer helping the National Guard fight the flood I had other things on my mind. All but the drowning at the end I know to be true. (Except for Benny Tacka's, the names are fictitious.)

"Midwife," "Old John Bush," and "The Priest and the Fiddler" were told to me by the late Robert Lyon of St. Marys. In 1986 I sat with the old German merchant on his front porch, watching the logging trucks roll by and drinking Straub Beer, made in the town. Fifty years after the fact, Lyon was able to draw from memory a decent map of property lines for 1918. Interestingly, most of the tales he told me were about women and birth. "Midwife" and "The Old Man" describe the primitive medical care available in the isolated logging camps and the mountains. Lyon's story about the priest points to the power struggle between the clergy, the town's founders, and secular interests.

Some stories are anonymous because of the sensitive nature of the material or because of faulty note taking. "Beer Robbery" comes from Donald R., an attorney, who still gets nervous telling the tale.

The Sheriff's Wife
A Schoolteacher

In most places in Pennsylvania, being a county sheriff is a good deal. Why, you get a salary, a house, a car, lots of people working for you, and your wife even gets

a salary if she cooks for the prisoners. See, in the rural
counties the sheriff's house is attached to the county
jail. It's a real good job.

In this county where I lived, we had a sheriff who
was always reelected. Let's call him Sheriff Wheeler
so's we don't hurt no feelings. He had been county
sheriff for twenty years. Here was a guy who knew
how to stay out of trouble. Mostly he'd just sit
around the jail and swap stories with the turnkey.
Folks respected him and even envied him because he
had a good job and a real nice wife and kids that
went on to college and all. But when he got into his
fifties, folks said he started getting uppity, started
thinking of his job as a permanent position.

That's about when he started getting the friskies.
Least, that's what Judge Hodges said. "When a fifty-
year-old man starts wearing Musk Oil and sporting a
gold necklace, you can tell he is coming down with a
bad case of the friskies," the judge told us.

"The friskies," Hodges said, "is when an old buck
starts going through the change of life. He knows
that in a year or so he'll be so old he won't grow no
horns at all, so he wants to get the most out of his
last season in rut. In short, the old buck acts like a
young buck and chases every doe on his side of the
hill. He might even chase 'em on the other side of
the hill. 'Bout that time, the old buck gets shot."

So the sheriff took up golf and joined a bigwigs'
country club downstate a ways. He told the missus it
was part of a business deal, that he needed the contact
with other big shots like himself. She went along with
it when he was gone most weekends. Sometimes he
wouldn't even come home on Saturday nights, but the

missus trusted him. After all, she figured, he'd been a good husband and father and even a grandfather all these years, so why should he quit now?

All that goodness must have gotten to the sheriff, because now that he was fifty he was horny as a hamster. Fact is, he was fooling around with a young lady at the country club. She wasn't near as pretty or as nice as his wife, but she was young and she made him feel young, and that was all he wanted.

When a well-known man in a small town starts cheating on his wife, his friends and his friends' wives can tell right away. Don't ask me how they know. They just know. It's one of the few really interesting and dangerous things outside of death that can happen in a small town. The cheating husband smiles a lot, he showers his wife with attention 'cause he feels guilty, and he's always on the go. It's the old buck's last mating season.

"Howdy, Sheriff. How's the golf game downstate?" his old-time friends would say.

"Getting your strokes in pretty regular, I'll bet," the judge said.

The sheriff, he just ignored them. He was sure that nobody knew nothing, when everybody knew everything, as they always do.

Then one day the sheriff's wife said to the judge's wife, "I think he's cheating on me."

"He is," the judge's wife said.

So they arranged to spy on him at his country club. To make it look like nothing was out of the ordinary, the sheriff's wife went with her friends to a big buffet they had at the country club. All the bigwigs were there. She knew the sheriff was there; she just wanted to see for herself how he spent his time.

There was a big wing-ding going on. People drinking cocktails and eating shrimp and pork sandwiches beside the pool. And it was all real polite and "So nice to see you."

Then she looked out over the fairway and saw the sheriff in a golf cart with one arm around his young girlfriend. She saw him stop the cart, lean over, and give his girlfriend a kiss. Then he got out.

Suddenly, from under the awning where the buffet was held, the sheriff's wife let out a horrible scream. "I'll kill you, you bastard," she yelled and ran out onto the fairway.

The sheriff's wife knocked tables and people over in her attack. He saw her coming at him through the crowd and across the grass. The girlfriend jumped and ran, but the sheriff was too stunned to move. When she got to him she started ripping at his shirt. Then he tried to push her away because she was crazy. But as he pushed her away, she grabbed him by the pockets of his pants and fell backwards. When she fell backwards, she ripped the front part of his pants right off. There was the sheriff with his pants down around his ankles looking dumbfounded at the hundred or so people on the patio. People began to laugh. It was too much. He grabbed up his pants and took off around the back of the clubhouse like a hobbled horse.

His wife went home with her friends. Of course, she was hysterical, so they stayed with her until she calmed down. When they finally left after she told them she was fine, she went down to the jail and ordered two deputies into the house. Now, over the years the sheriff's wife had earned a position of power equal to the sheriff, so when she said, "Hop," you jumped. She ordered the deputies to carry all of the sheriff's personal effects downstairs and put them out in the street along the curb. Now, this town was small, and before long every subnatural, every slackjaw, and every drooler within five miles was out there pondering the mystery of sheriff Wheeler's favorite rocker, his dresser piled high with his clothes and shoes, and even his guns. Huck and Buck Zook (they were twins) had concluded that the sheriff was *giving* his things away to his friends, until Deputy Chinky Dunham pushed them away.

Then somebody started shooting upstairs in the sheriff's house. "Oh, my God, she's killed herself," Chinky said, and ran upstairs. In fact, about forty people ran upstairs, since the idea that Sheriff Wheeler's wife was shooting herself was truly a historical event, perhaps *the* historical event of the century. They were relieved and disappointed to find Mrs. Wheeler in the bedroom pumping rounds from the forty-four she held in her hand into the bed where she and the sheriff had slept.

The Zooks and the Jollies and the Undertucks and the other subnaturals all agreed that this *was* a historical event that ranked with Prince Farrington's visit to the county back in 1928 when the famous bootlegger drove into town with a truck with a fake extra gas tank full of eighty gallons of the finest whiskey anybody had ever tasted. Eck Zook had gotten so drunk he couldn't find his ass from third base.

The sheriff didn't even bother to run for reelection. His wife remained in town with the pity and good feelings of everyone on her side. The sheriff turned up as a used car salesman down in Cambria County. His former friends, the lawyers and doctors of the town, were scared by what happened to him, but they pretended to take it all as a big joke and they never stopped telling and retelling the golf club incident. The judge kept on saying, "You see, boys, the sheriff just couldn't keep his pants on."

Uncle Bish and the Beets
John LaRose, Lock Haven

I grew up Mennonite around Middleburg. It seemed like a normal life to me until my real father died, and then my mother married a man from Texas who was working on a gas pipeline. He liked the land up here. We were shunned, more or less. Even though she would go to the church and drag me along, all the brethren were kind of standoffish, even her sisters. It hurt her a lot.

Over the years it kind of wore off. She could go to the social but not the religious events. Everybody got used to it. They don't like outsiders knowing about their ways. That's why they get so upset when one of them leaves. They fear the ridicule. 'Course, once you're out, it does look kind of funny, looking back at them and all. That's the part they don't like.

I remember the kids bringing their lunch to school every day, sandwiches wrapped in wax paper in brown bags. After lunch the little kids would wipe off the wax paper, fold it back up, and put it back in

117

the bag. That was their paper and bag for the week, you see. And at night they would sit in the living room and chat with visitors in the dark because it would save on whatever they were burning.

And I remember Uncle Bish and the beets. He loved beets. Every summer he grew a big patch of red beets and in the fall he would turn them out and clean and can them. One year he was living with us while he was doing all the canning. He couldn't afford to live alone any more, so he stopped shunning my mother. It was cheaper not to shun her, and she gladly took him in. Well, we kids sliced and boiled, pickled and canned beets for two days with Uncle Bish. He was so happy the beets came so good that he had to taste some of every can we put up. He must have eaten two or three quarts of beets.

We heard Uncle Bish scream next morning before breakfast, and we ran outside as Daddy was carrying Bish out to the car. He was moaning and crying the whole time. As Dad turned the car around in the driveway, Uncle Bish hung his head out, rolled his sick eyes at the kids and said, "Billy, I'm a dead man. You'll never see me alive again. I hemorrhaged inside and all the blood is coming out of me when I take a piss. Pray for me."

Two hours later, my dad and Bish came home drunk. We could hear them whooping and hollering as the car came down the farm road. We were all standing there when they got out. Bish was laughing and singing and tears were streaming down his face. We ran over to him and he hugged all five of us kids at once. "It was only the beet juice, children, only the beet juice. I wasn't pissing blood at all, like I thought. Oh, no. It was only that I'd eaten two quarts of canned beets yesterday that made my pee go red. It's a warning from God, but I'm not going to die."

After that, Uncle Bish never shunned us again.

Praise the Lord and Fill the Tank
Larry Miller, Wellsboro

I met Skeeter Smith on the day the old Italian lady was brought to trial. I remember because she had taken a shot at me with a twenty-two. We laughed about it later, the officer and I. She said we had no right to be on her property because she was born on the *Queena Maria* and was therefore a citizen of this country.

Anyway, after the trial, Jim Carlson, then assistant district attorney, came up to me and said that one of Christ's Disciples was down on the front steps of the courthouse trying to buy gas. It was my job to deal with these people. Down I went and there he was, a tall, dark, lanky, bedraggled Jesus freak.

"Hi," I said. "I'm Larry Miller and I understand you are trying to buy some gas here at the courthouse."

"Praise the Lord, yes, hallelujah. I'm preaching the word in Jesus' name, and I'm a pilgrim passing through. I have no money to pay, but the Lord will see to my needs as he does for the sparrow in the field."

"Well, look, why don't you come around the corner to the clinic and we'll get you some gas there—maybe give you a bite to eat," I said.

"Whatever the Lord wills, so be it. He will deliver

119

me from my affliction and provide the gas for me to drive to New York State to see my aged parents. His will be done."

So we drove over to the mental health clinic, and he came along real willingly. Inside, I made him a sandwich and chatted with him about his travels.

"Been preaching the Word all over Georgia, been in Baltimore, and now I'm headed home. I used to be a paranoid schizophrenic but the Lord has cured me—can't you tell?" he said.

"Oh, it's obvious to me," I said.

The psychiatrist talked to him for a while and decided that he was well enough to drive home. "How far away is home?" the doctor asked Skeeter.

"Fifteen gallons is all I need to get there," he said.

Meanwhile, I called his home since he had given me the number. "Hello, Mr. Smith."

"Yes."

"This is Larry Miller down in Tioga County, Pennsylvania. We have your boy Skeeter here at the mental health clinic and we want to know if it is all right to send him home."

"Hallelujah! Praise be to Jesus. The Lord works in strange ways. He has returned to us our boy after using him in His divine ways," said the boy's father. "He called Skeeter out one month ago and now he is returning him to us. Hallelujah!"

Then I said, "He needs some gas to come home, but he is out of money. What do you want us to do?"

"Do? Just trust in the Lord. Buy the boy a tank of gas and send him home. I'll mail you a check today. Trust in the Lord."

The psychiatrist said Skeeter was OK to drive, and

so, trusting in the Lord, I took him down to the gas station, pumped out fifteen dollars for him and wished him luck. Just as he was leaving, though, I noticed a bottle of wine on the front seat of the car.

"Skeeter, here let me put that under the front so the police don't think you're drinking and driving," I said as I reached in and hid the bottle.

Skeeter thought for a minute and then reached down grabbed the bottle and plopped it right up on the dashboard.

"Practice not deceit before God nor thy fellow man," he said, and roared off.

That was the last I ever saw of Skeeter Smith, the agent of the Lord—*and* the last I ever saw of my fifteen dollars. Praise Jesus.

Flying Baby Jesus
Michael Martin, Roaring Spring

Now, the folks in the little white clapboard churches out in the country like to do it up big for Christmas. They like a special something for the holiday season. Most times they'll get them some nice china dolls from people, and the ladies will make manger clothes for the dolls. They'll dress up a Mary and a Joseph and the Three Wise Men and the whole deal.

One year one of them churches up Beech Creek had a dog dolled up to look like a sheep. They stuck cotton balls all over this mangy dog and put it outside the manger. It lay there all right, but it kept

121

on scratchin'. The little kids would point and say, "Mommy, why is that sheep scratchin'?"

Anyway, this one church had a special china Jesus it used every year in the manger. It was about yea big and looked like a tiny white baby. Had a little ring on its back so it could be hung up—don't ask me why—but that's what give Delmo the idea that started all the trouble with the flying baby Jesus.

See, Delmo Waffle is my brother. Now, Delmo is the type that always has to try something new. When he saw the china baby Jesus, he wanted to do something big—something folks would remember. So this is what he done.

Every Christmas we pull the pulpit forward to the center of the altar, turn it around, and make the manger scene in the hollow back of the pulpit. Baby Jesus goes right in the center and all the others around him.

But what Delmo said was, "What I want to do is run a wire from the manger up into the choir loft. When the time comes during the service, I'll use a thread to let it down slowly. Why, it'll look real impressive, I know. Folks will be real surprised, He was right about that.

Well, we went along with him, and when the day came only a few folks knew about what was going to happen. "Where's the baby Jesus?" they'd all ask.

At a certain time, after the first hymns and before the sermon, Delmo started sliding the baby Jesus on down. Now, Elsie Bayard was the organist, and she knew nothing about the flying Jesus. When this thing slid down toward her from high up in the loft, she caught sight of it out of the corner of her eye. Was she surprised? You bet! She thought it was a bat. She picked up her hymn book and swatted it. That broke Delmo's thread he used to slow the flying Jesus down, so off it went sliding down that wire toward the pulpit.

Well, the next thing that happened was Elsie's sister Peena heard Elsie shriek, and she jumped up and looked around to see what was the matter. That's when the flying baby Jesus caught her upside the head and knocked her colder than a creek rock.

That didn't slow it down none, though. It kept on flying right for the manger. Only trouble was, it didn't stop there. It went through the back of the pulpit and hit the preacher right between the legs. He let out a great moan, put one hand up in the air and the other between his legs. Gabby Dilli, who is deaf as a fencepost, thought the preacher was calling for testimony, so he jumped up and began to praise the Lord.

Yessir, for a while there it was a regular three-ring circus. But finally they got it straightened out, and I can tell you that's the last time they'll have that flying baby Jesus in that church.

Shotlight
Dick Sassaman, Sterling Run

Two young brothers lived out in the country south of Emporium in an area just loaded with deer. Now, these brothers would shoot deer like they were jackrabbits in Australia. A mile from their house, the boys found an old abandoned barn with

bays opening from three sides of the loft. In the
fields below grew clover and buckwheat, so at night
the deer came to graze by the hundreds. These young
men got their kicks this way: they would sit up in
that barn at night looking out over a good half mile
of deer-filled field on each side, and they would wait
until a car came along. Likely as not the car, was
going to spotlight. The boys got ready as soon as the
spotlight started beaming around the field. When the
light landed on a deer—*Kapow!*—a shot would ring
out, and the deer would fall to the ground. The poor
people in the car. They would turn the light out, roll
up the window and speed away. They must have
wondered what was in that spotlight that killed the
deer. Think about it. You shine a spotlight on a deer
and—*Pow!*—down it goes.

Deputy Fish Warden
Dick Sassaman, Sterling Run

My father and his brothers were going to fish the
Sinnemahoning one spring day, so they drove
down as far as they could go on the dirt road until
they hit a muddy spot. They decided they would get
out here and let one of my cousins drive the car
back. Now, the boy was about fifteen, too young for
a driver's license, but it was a dirt road in the woods,
so no one thought anything of it. The boy turned
around and headed back up the dirt road. A few
minutes later, the grownups heard someone from up

there yell, "Freeze! Get out and put your hands in the air!"

The men ran to see what was going on, but my father went sneaking off into the bushes. When the men got to the car, they saw a deputy fish warden pointing a gun at the boy. The warden looked at them and said, "This kid's driving on state land without a driver's license. He's under arrest."

The men started pleading with him and even threatening him for such a stupid arrest, but he wouldn't budge. While they were arguing with him, my father slipped out of the bushes, inched up on the deputy, and grabbed the gun from his hand. Then he emptied all the shells in the bushes and handed the gun back to the overzealous deputy and said, "Now, you go back into town and get your superior officer and come back here to arrest this boy and me. We'll be waiting right here."

The deputy drove away and never came back. They say deputies do the dumbest things because they're trying too hard to get promoted to full-time warden.

Boy in the Woods
Norm Erickson, Emporium

Now I am retired, but I was a game warden in Pennsylvania for over thirty years and this is one of the strangest experiences I ever had. It happened about fifteen years ago right here in this area near Emporium. One day I was driving the Scout on a lonely dirt road in the state game lands. There's a few cabins up that way, and I was supposed to keep an eye on them. Well, I drove past one and noticed the front door ajar, so I stopped and came up to the cabin. I looked in the door and there was a boy of about fifteen with a backpack loading up on food from the cabin. I drew my gun and made him put his hands up. Then I frisked him and made him lie down on the floor. Then I interrogated him. We'd had a lot of robberies in cabins up this way, and I figured I had the guy we were looking for. I said to the kid, "Now, what do you have to say for yourself?"

He looked up at me then, and I noticed that he had tears in his eyes. There was something about him that I hadn't understood from the start. Then he said, "Mister, I'm no outlaw. I'm retarded."

Then I recognized him. He was Fred Johnson's son Billy, grown almost to a man—and this was Fred's cabin. After I apologized and made friends with the young man, I asked him what he was doing way out here in the woods, and he told me about himself and how he lived.

Maybe Billy was more of an epileptic than a retarded person—I just don't know. But he hated school because he would have seizures and the kids would tease him and he couldn't do the work even in the special classes. Now, his Dad had the cabin way out in the middle of nowhere, and that is where Billy said he felt happy. Being around more than a few people made him nervous and caused him to have seizures. When he turned sixteen, Billy told his father that he wanted to try to live in the woods, to try to survive on his own during the summer months. He begged his father so much that Fred let him go. As long as he stayed close to the cabin where there was food, Fred figured he would be all right. Billy was so determined to live like a survivalist, his father let him go.

Well, after talking to him in the cabin that day, I began to kind of look out for him. 'Course, I was all over the forest all the time. I'd ask folks if they'd seen the boy. "Oh, yes, he came through Dent's Run yesterday. Came out to the store for some food, then crossed the road and headed on up the mountain going south. He looked good. Always a smile."

That's the truth. He was a smily kid, Billy was. I crossed him late one August day on the Susquehanna Trail, and we sat and talked for a while. He told me he could live by eating insects and roots. He showed me a survival book in his backpack. He couldn't read it. He showed me rope he had made with his own hands out of deerskin. It wasn't good for much, but it was amazing that he had made it at all.

Billy told me he hadn't had any seizures in a long time and that he was feeling better. After I spoke to him that day on the Susquehanna Trail I didn't see him for a few weeks. When I asked about him, nobody had seen him, not even his Dad. We all got kind of concerned, what with his seizures and all. Then I heard a policeman found him on a mountain road over in Clearfield County, and he was in bad shape. So I went to visit Billy, and he told me what had happened.

Seems he had wandered far away from the cabin to a place I have been only once—Mosquito Creek. It's a wild snaky place where nobody ever goes. He was trying to test himself by going to the roughest place

127

he could find. Well, the seizure came over him while he was in the woods, and it lasted for days. He just lay there, he said, and he couldn't move, he had such a bad fit. He could hear music, people singing, and he could see boats and buildings that weren't there. That fit nearly killed him. Then it just quit. When he came to, he felt better, so he pulled himself together and came out of the woods.

Now, the strangest thing is this: after that, Billy got better—he almost became normal. He learned to read and to drive a car. He drove to Buffalo last week—can you imagine that? It is just the strangest thing I ever heard.

The State Trooper and the Turkey
Norm Erickson, Emporium

This happened about ten years ago. Everybody around here remembers it because it was so unusual and later become such a big deal. One day a man was cutting his grass at his home a few miles outside of town. His house was on a rise above the road and he could see a half mile down the road in either direction. While he was bending down to fix his mower, he noticed a state police car stopped about a hundred yards down the road. He saw a trooper get out of the car, take out a twenty-two and aim across the field. Then the man saw a flock of turkeys in the field. He had seen them often. Next thing, the trooper shot, and one of the turkeys fell. The man was shocked. It was the middle of summer and the trooper was in uniform. Killing a turkey like that was illegal. Then he watched the policeman run out into the field, grab the turkey, and stash it in the roots of a big oak tree.

Quickly the man went back to mowing his lawn and pretended he had seen nothing. The cop drove on up to the house, stopped, and asked the man if he had seen any rattlesnakes lately. Also, had he heard any shots? "No," the man said.

"Well if you did hear a shot, it was just my car backfiring," the trooper said. Then he drove away.

The man wrote down the license number of the police car. Then he telephoned the game warden. That's me. I came right on out, and together we found the turkey. We had him cold. What a fool thing to do. Now I had to arrest him, and I knew he wasn't going to like it. He was a sergeant. And I knew all hell would break loose in the two state agencies. The rule is to keep our noses clean and to help each other do this. The secret code said that I should just drop it, but no way was I going to do that. The guy was an on-duty cop and he was poaching and I was going to fry his ass.

So I drove into town until I found his car where I knew it would be—at the diner. He spent a lot of time drinking coffee. I went in and said I needed to talk to him about something outside. "What is it now?" he said in a carefree way.

"I want to talk to you about the turkey you shot this morning," I said.

"What are you talking about? It ain't turkey-hunting season," he said.

"I'm talking about the one you shot out on the

road this morning with the twenty-two. I've got a witness and I've got the turkey in the Scout," I said.

Well, the man's life just crumbled right before him. He started shaking and crying, and panic came over him. "Oh, my God, I'm ruined. What can I do, Norm?" he said as he grabbed on to my arms.

"You should admit to it right now and sign a field receipt. Get it off your mind," I told him.

But he wouldn't do that, because he was convinced somehow the troopers would make it go away. And they tried. I got letters from all kinds of state representatives and agency chiefs, some of them from within the Game Commission. They said I was hurting the police and the Game Commission, that I was a stubborn old cuss, and that I should be more humane. I didn't see it that way at all. I never gave an inch.

Now, the state trooper was my neighbor, and he used to come over and ask, "Have you heard anything?" and I would tell him no. Oh, it was sticky. Finally they had a hearing down in Montoursville—a court-martialing. They suspended him, and then they transferred him. He is still with the state police, but the incident set him back. No one is above the law—especially the lawman.

Frosty the Poacher
Norm Erickson, Emporium

Now, there is one poacher I will always remember. He was almost like a wayward son to

me. He couldn't obey the law. He'd shoot just for
the fun of shooting. He lived to hunt. Frosty was
his name. Almost pure Seneca Indian from the
reservation over in Salamanca he was. Frosty's idea
of a good time was cruising the forest roads after dark
trying to shoot as many deer as he could. He had
been in jail for it, he had his license permanently
revoked by the state, and still he did it. And the
more I arrested him, the more he became my friend.
There was no way I couldn't like the guy. These are
just a few of the things he did.

Frosty and his buddies would follow me on my
rounds in the evening with their lights out. They
thought I didn't know. Then they would follow me
back to my house, and when they were sure I was in for
the night they would go out and start jacklighting. Of
course, I would be only bluffing, but it fooled them
more than once. Next thing, I'd be following them.
They were like kids, and maybe I was too.

One time I came upon some guys jacklighting in a
cornfield and they shot at the Scout. Put a bullet
right through the back window. I been shot at in the
war, and it made me angry. So I came after them. I
pulled my gun on them and said, "Who's doing the
shooting?" I walked right up and popped one of
those guys in the jaw, and I got in a lot of trouble
for that. Frosty was one of them.

"Gosh, Norm, we didn't know you was in the car
or we wouldn't have shot at you. Come on and arrest
us because we're guilty as hell," Frosty said.

Frosty had a woman and she was ugly. They lived
together in a shack, and some black people lived
in a shack next to them. Well, Frosty's woman got

pregnant and when she had the baby it was pretty clear that Frosty wasn't the father because it was a black child. Frosty was pretty angry and he went around telling his friends this: "I'm willing to overlook it this once, but it better not happen again."

Now, I was always a bit of a hothead and sometimes I would do things my own way and the Game Commission wouldn't quite like it. Five hunters from Niagara came here every year and always gave me a hard time. I had arrested one of them for hunting without a license, and they had it in for me. So one day I stopped in the woods and did a routine check of their licenses. They started cursing me out—calling me a bum and other things. I went to the biggest loudmouth and said, "Let's you and me go and have it out right now. I'll forget I'm a warden and we'll just step over here in the clearing and fight it out with bare knuckles."

Well, that shut him up, but later he filed a complaint which forced the Game Commission to hold a public hearing about me in Emporium. All my enemies were supposed to get up and badmouth me in front of my boss. They all chickened out. They didn't have the guts to say anything. Instead, Frosty got up and said, "I can say a few things about Norm here. I know him pretty well. He's the only warden with guts enough to arrest me and he's arrested me fourteen times. He's the best warden in the state. Take my word for it: I've poached in every county in northern Pennsylvania."

After Frosty had his say, nobody else wanted to speak. They figured he had said about all there was to say and they just forgot about the whole thing.

The Great Flood
Benny Tacka and Dave Darby, Blossburg

The Tioga River had jumped its banks and flooded the tiny town of Blossburg so many times over the past hundred years that the state finally built a dike between the town and the river. The town felt a lot safer after they built the dike. The state and the engineers and the townspeople had a big town meeting after the dike was complete. The engineers said, "The kind of flood that could break through this dike comes only once in a hundred years."

When the people of Blossburg heard this, many understood it to mean that every hundred years a big flood would come and break through the dike. So they asked the engineer at the meeting if he meant they would have flood protection for eighty years or so. He smiled and said, "At least for that long."

Next day, the state officials and the engineers were all gone. But the people thought more and more about what they had heard. Finally, led by the mayor and the funeral director of the town, they came up with this formula:

Last big flood	1955
Between big floods	+ 100 years
Next big flood	2055
This year	− 1969
Flood-free years	86

They knew it wasn't totally foolproof, but they said

you could pretty well bank on it. Eighty-six flood-free years was a long time.

All this impressed Jes Droleski so much that he bought two acres down by the river and began building the dream home that he and his wife had waited for for so long. Six months later, they moved into their new ranch house. They had sunk all their savings into it. It had aluminum siding, Anderson windows, a Woodmode kitchen—the works. Jes said, "Not too shabby for a dumb Polack from the foundry."

Things went along fine until the spring of 1972. She rained for a week to beat hell, and the river rose to the top of the dike and stayed there. You could hear the river just humming out beyond Jes's backyard. He had a measuring stick he drove into the dike to watch her rise and fall. He didn't seem worried, but he did start asking then about the hundred years business.

Benny Tacka told him the hundred years was a crock dreamed up by the engineers and that the river would do what it had a mind to do—no more and no less. This worried Jes. That night he and Irma went up to the Polish church in Morris Run and lit candles.

Next day, down at Ray's Diner, he told his friends, "I'm still banking on science. There ain't going to be a flood 'cause there ain't one due. Look outside, the sun is coming out."

It was true. The sun came out for a few hours that day, but later on, it turned dark and rained buckets. Four inches fell in four hours. That was Agnes. She put half the state under water. We all knew Jes was going under, so we went down to help.

It was just awful. Had to open all the doors and windows to let the river run through to keep the house from washing away.

Jes? He changed right there before our eyes. He said, "Boys, that rivers got almost a hundred years to flow by here without coming into my backyard and up my ass. Why does it have to pick this year? It's such a goddamn long shot. No, sir. It ain't a fair flood. Something's against me, and I know it."

By the time we got some clothes and furniture out, the river was a big brown roaring train sucking everything along—cars, houses, coffins. It scared us to look at it. It was ripping away half the town. Went on for three days.

Later, after the water went down, we started digging folks out. The mud is the worst part because it hardens like cement. The flooded town looked like it had been bombed. It was a wonderment. And the people seemed happy because they were running around and grabbing you and laughing and shouting. Then you would realize they weren't happy—they were nuts.

Including Jes Droleski. His house was a terrible mess, with two feet of mud covering his living room. The dike had washed away. What was once a nice grassy wall was now a slope down to the river. We pumped and dug and scrubbed, but we could never get that house back where it was. Of course, it ruined Jes. He became permanently depressed.

He felt God had done it to him, and he wanted to get even. He grew skinny, gloomy, and bitter, and he said the government and science had let him down. Finally, the government gave him some of

135

that flood money. "Just a bribe to shut me up," Jes said.

So he would wander into Ray's Diner and talk to the boys. He would say, "What I can't understand is that hundred years. If it's supposed to last for a hundred years, how come I get wiped out in three?"

Finally, the boys decided to cure him with the truth. Benny said, "Jes they meant that sometime *during* the hundred years a big flood is going to come along. It could come at any time. And in this case it did. Fact is, you were a fool to take the experts at their word. Science, government—shit—they don't know nothing. Besides, everybody around here knows—a big flood comes every *twenty-five years*."

Benny went on, "Jes, you have had all the bad luck you are going to have, so loosen up and relax. Let go of that river and it will leave ya alone." After that, Jes changed. He started living again. Now, Ben said after a tragedy like Jes's, you will avoid bad luck for about ten years. That was about right for Jes Droleski. Ten years after Agnes he had a heart attack and died. He keeled over in the river and floated down to Putnam Park. But those were ten good years.

Liquor Control Board
Howard Kistner, Montoursville

I was with the State Police for twenty-seven years, and I was the chief county detective for Lycoming County starting in 1961. I worked with

the district attorneys—Henry Hager and Paul
Reeder. I saw some strange things and I saw some
sad sights.

Back then, we had the Highway Patrol and the
State Police. The State Police were founded in 1905,
and they worked with traffic, crimes, bootleggers,
and such. The Liquor Control Board didn't come
into existence until around 1933. The Highway
Patrol began in 1923, and they wore caps and big
badges and rode Indian motorcycles.

When I entered the State Police Training
School in Hershey in 1932, it was like the army.
We did a lot of drills, rode horses—oh, yes,
we were a mounted force, back then. When the
Depression came, the state couldn't afford to bring
in another class, so we stayed on to take care of
the horses after we graduated. During the day we'd
patrol clear down to the Maryland line. And this
is how what I'm going to tell you came to
happen.

We were trying out one of the first car radios. It
was a one-way radio. Sounds funny, I know. They
would call you from headquarters and then you
would have to get to a phone and call in to find out
what was what. They were trying it out in Lancaster
County, and one night I was patroling with an
officer—I was just a rookie then—down along the
Maryland border. We were waving over cars and
trucks and inspecting them.

McCulloch—that was his name—and I were there
at the crossroads below Quarryville, and we saw
truck lights coming south in the distance. We started
flagging him down, but he just hit the gas and

137

swerved off a side road that was a shortcut to
Maryland. So we took off after him.

Now, this was one of those "Pinchot roads," and
by that I mean just a ten-foot-wide dirt road that had
just been paved. Yessir. They said Pinchot took the
farmer out of the dirt, because when he was governor
of Pennsylvania he paved the farm roads.

Anyway, we tried to take off after the truck, and
we just sat there spinning our wheels until I got out
and pushed. The grass was wet, you see. Pretty soon,
we started gaining on the truck, but then it stopped
and the driver took off into a cornfield. Four rows
and a man is gone forever in a cornfield, so
McCulloch and I let him go.

The truck was filled with moonshine. There were
five-gallon kegs made of wood with metal hoops, and
five-gallon cans. There were about twenty of each. It
was quite a haul for a rookie to be in on. So
McCulloch drove the truck and I drove the car back
to the barracks, and we locked up the truck and
turned in the keys and went to bed.

Now, the Liquor Control Board had just been
organized, but they still didn't have many men or a
full organization. The barracks called them in, and
this was their first load of moonshine. It was the
brass of the Liquor Control Board, and I could tell
they didn't know what they were doing. They told
me to initial all those cans and kegs, so I did. They
stored them in the mechanical units and in the
stables. You could tell they didn't just want to
dump the stuff. Word got around that it was top-
grade whiskey—maybe some of Prince Farrington's
stuff.

Well, they had a big ceremony and they took pictures, but I know the Liquor Control Board only destroyed two kegs of that whiskey. Just enough to make a smell. This was grade A stuff and it was a hundred and twenty proof. Then it just began to disappear.

One day, the head of the barracks called McCulloch and me into his office, "I want to know if you two guys dumped any of that whiskey off in the woods—sort of a secret store?"

McCulloch looked him in the eye, held up his hand, and said, "Sir, I swear to you that we brought all the hooch in. We didn't hide any of it."

"Well, why didn't you, you damn fool?" the barracks sergeant said.

The Midwife
Robert Lyon, St. Marys

When I was a lad of sixteen, my mother sent me out to collect for St. Vincent's Catholic Church here in St. Marys. Most everybody was Catholic back then. I called at a house where they spoke Tyrolean German, and I could barely understand the lady. She looked at me and pulled me into the house. I began to understand that she knew who I was and that she had something she wanted to tell me, so when she sat me down and served me hot chocolate and cookies, I didn't protest. Then she began:

"Edwin, your mother was the dearest person in the

139

world to me. When I came over from the Tyrol some years ago, we came up here to St. Marys. It was the end of the world here, deep in the woods and cold, but there was lots of work, and a nice German community. So I got a job as a cook in one of the logging camps. The camps were portable even back then. We would move every three or four months. Sometimes the camp would be on a train. Four women would cook in a big camp and two in the smaller camps. The men always treated the ladies respectfully.

"Before long, I had married and was expecting a child. I was still in the camp. It was winter and I didn't think the child would come for another few weeks. I was wrong. I went into labor and they sent for a doctor. The doctors were all out on other calls, so they went to your mother. She was in her twenties, but she had assisted the old midwives and the doctors at many births. She agreed to come, though the way was long. Two loggers put her in the sleigh and headed for the camp along Toby's Run. By the time they got there, the snow was falling hard. I needed her then.

"She delivered my daughter who I named after her. The child had hurt me, and I couldn't get up for three days or work for seven. All that time your mother stayed. She cooked and cleaned for the loggers and helped me take care of the child. She brought such happiness to the camp.

"When it came time for her to go, I said to her, 'How much do I owe you?'"

"'Nothing,' she said, 'Just pray for me.'"

140

"Now you understand why your mother means so much to me."

Old John Bush
Robert Lyon, St. Marys

We had two German doctors in St. Marys, a husband-and-wife team named Muller. They were good doctors. Sometimes they got so busy traveling around to see sick people they didn't have time for patients in their office. They had a secretary and she would try to keep the impatient ones calm. It wasn't always easy.

Old John Bush lived up on Charles Street. He was a mean old cuss. He hated everybody, especially the kids, so they would always tease him. They would steal his newspaper, lean milk bottles full of water against his door, ring his doorbell, and then just run. Anything to torment him. One day he went to the doctor to get a checkup. But both doctors were busy delivering babies in Ridgeway.

The doctors' secretary told John Bush that one of the doctors might be back around noon, so he came back at noon. Then she told the old man the doctors would be back around five P.M. This made the man mad. "Why can't one of them be here now?"

"Because they both have confinements today," the secretary said.

"A what?" John Bush said.

The secretary explained it to him. "A woman is

141

having a baby and the doctor stays with her until it is over. Sometimes it takes a long time."

This interested old Bush. "How much does it cost to have a baby?"

"It costs ten dollars," the girl said.

"Oh, my God, that's awful," said John Bush.

"Unless there's a problem, and then it's fifteen dollars," the secretary said.

"Fifteen? I can't believe it."

Now, the secretary saw where this was going, and she saw a way to get rid of the old cuss. "And if the doctor has to use instruments to deliver the baby it can cost twenty-five dollars. And—"

Here John Bush interrupted her. He looked like he'd been hit with the mallet they used to stun the pigs. He forgot what he wanted to see the doctor about. Suddenly he felt fine. He headed for the door of the doctors' office. This talk of babies and of the money it cost to bring them into the world had distracted him. As he walked out of the office, the secretary heard him say, "My God, what an expensive sport!"

The Priest and the Fiddler
Robert Lyon, St. Marys

Father Mahan was a priest at St. Leo's in Ridgeway and he was a go-getter. A big strong Irishman he was. Oh, the priests had their way back then. They were educated, and they knew how to get what was good for the town. The whole area was

German and Catholic. St. Marys was laid out by the Benedictines in the 1800s. People have always gone along with the priests because they have never let us down.

Anyway, Father Mahan organized this big fair to raise money for the church. It was called a kermess—a sort of harvest festival like they have in Germany. They would hold this frolic in McGuinness's Hall, a big two-story building. The church bazaar would be held on the ground floor. Later on, the big dance would begin up on the second floor. Now McBride's orchestra was going to play for that dance, and they were the best around. The young kids could hardly wait for the music to begin.

Well Father Mahan had personally organized the bazaar this year. He wanted the church to make a lot of money. He made it a moral obligation to spend lots of money at the bazaar, and he even stood at the door leading up to the dance, sort of blocking the way until everybody had run out of dough. The wheel of fortune, the coin-toss, the baseball throw, and the gypsy fortuneteller—they were all big moneymakers. Mrs. Holstein was disguised as Glenda the Gypsy.

Upstairs, McBride's men were tuning up. They were supposed to start at nine sharp, and they didn't want to be there all night. When people heard the music, it was like bees to the flower: young and old, men and women stampeded up the stairs to the dance floor. They were tired of spending their money on Mrs. Holstein's misty predictions of romance. They wanted the real thing—somebody real to swing

143

in their arms and to promenade home—and they didn't want to pay for it.

But Father Mahan was used to having his own way. He wasn't ready for the dance to begin— besides, he wouldn't be dancing, anyway. To him, the dance was like the moneylenders in the temple and he meant to drive them out, at least until he was ready for them to begin.

He told McBride to hold off, but McBride rosined up his bow and then started in to shuffle, and all his musicians came in for "Soldier's Joy." Father Mahan turned red in the face. Pacing right over to McBride, he started grabbing his elbow, knowing full well that even a mighty fiddler like McBride cannot play with a six-foot monsignor riding on his arm. And Father Mahan saying, "Wait, wait, the dance doesn't start until the bazaar is over, and the bazaar isn't over until I say so."

And McBride shouting, "Take your hand off my bowing arm. The dance starts now—priest or no damn priest."

And together they struggled while McBride's bow skidded across the strings making a screeching sound that made all the dancers on the floor laugh. Everybody in the room was dancing while the priest struggled with McBride. They watched, but they did not stop dancing.

Then McBride leaped back and said, "Enough of this here. I'll meet you tomorrow at noon in the park and we'll settle this if you're man enough."

"The park suits me fine," said the priest. "God forgive me, but I'm going to beat the face off of you,

you ballroom bungler. I'll teach you to rob the coffers of Holy Mother Church."

That was the end of it. McBride knew better than to fight a priest in the town of St. Marys. He'd have had a curse on him if he lifted a hand. And Father Mahan knew it. Oh, he made a big show of going down to the park next day, but in his heart he was grateful to McBride for not being there. Then McBride did a brave and humble thing: he went to confession and asked to be forgiven. Father Mahan was so surprised that he asked McBride to forgive *him.* After that they were friends. But McBride and the whole town learned an important lesson from all that: when a man of God is earning money for the church, stay out of his way. It's every bit God's work as are funerals, baptisms, and marriages.

A Horse Named Red
A Schoolteacher

I live way out in the country, and I have to drive on a narrow road that winds through cornfields for a couple of miles. This one night I was coming home, the corn was high and the evening warm, so I had the windows open on the Honda. All of a sudden, I heard hoofbeats thudding alongside the car. When I looked over, I saw the legs and the belly of a large horse running along next to my car. It must have come out of the cornfield.

The horse running beside the car spooked me. I

slowed down, and it slowed down, I sped up and it
sped up. Finally, I just came to a stop. Then the
horse walked out into the headlights and looked back
at me as if to say, "What's the matter, don't you
want to play any more?" Then it trotted off into the
corn rows.

I drove on down the road slowly, expecting to be
jumped by the horse again. I pulled into a driveway
at a nearby farmhouse. A light was on in the living
room, and as I walked up the front steps of the old
farmhouse I could see a very old lady sitting in front
of the TV watching "Hee Haw" and drinking a can
of beer. I remember she had blue slippers on and a
yellow terrycloth bathrobe. Her hair was in shock.
Somehow I knew she had to be the owner of this
wayward horse. She opened the door and said,
"What d'ya want this time of night?"

"Sorry to bother you, but there's a horse loose and
I almost hit it," I replied.

She looked at me and said, "What kind of a
horse?"

"It's a big brownish horse and it ran alongside my
car for a ways, scared the life out of me."

"Oh Jesus, it's Red again, chasing cars. I thought I
had him locked in the barn for the night, but that
horse can get out of a knothole. He's an escape
artist. And what does he do when he gets out? He
chases cars. That's Red's big thing, you know,
chasing cars. He thought he was chasing you, scaring
you off. He's just a big bully. He lurks in the
cornfields and then—*Pow!*—he's out on you and got
you scared. Tried to cut you off too, didn't he?"

Then she walked to the edge of the front porch,

put two fingers in her lips and let fly a shrill whistle. Then she cupped her hands and bellowed, "Ray-ed, Ray-ed," so hard I could see the little veins popping up in her temples. Soon the horse loped into the yard. He trotted over to her with his head down to take his medicine.

The old woman raised her arm and pointed at the horse. "Red, I thought I told you never to chase cars again. Scaring this poor woman like that. Now get the hell in the barn and stay there for the rest of the night."

Then she looked at me and winked, "He's a good horse, you know, but I got to be firm with him. He won't bother you again. When it comes to chasing cars, well, Red just can't help himself."

Beer Robbery
Donald R., State College

I won't tell you my name or the place where this happened because we committed a crime and they may still be looking for us. My best friend and I were prelaw students in a respected liberal arts college. During the summer we had easy jobs as lifeguards, so we used to go out drinking and partying every night. One night we got very drunk and wandered into a bar where a band played loud, horrible rock music.

By nature, my friend John was very cautious; he would never do anything wrong. But that night he was a different person. Returning from a trip to the men's room, he said to me, "You know, they've got

cases of beer stacked up to the roof in the back
room?"

"So what?" I said.

"Well, there's an alley right outside the back door
and nothing between it and the beer but a little
screen door," he said.

"So what are you getting at?" I asked.

"I just unlocked the screen door. Let's drive your
Volkswagon around back and up the alley and steal
some beer."

I was so drunk it sounded good to me. We pushed
through the madhouse bar with its bad music and
stepped into the hot summer night. The owners of
the bar were so busy making money and the night
was so hot, they had forgotten about security. To our
drunken minds, that beer was already ours: TAKE
ME was printed on every case. As we drove the bug
down the narrow alley behind the bar to the open
door, it did not occur to us that there was no
turnaround. In our getaway, we would be *backing out.*
But we parked the car, walked around the screen
door, and casually started unloading cases of beer
into the VW. We filled the bug up so high that one
case was sticking through the sunroof. We backed
out slowly, scratching bushes and even a fence. Still
we felt no fear, anxiety, or nervousness.

We lived only two blocks away, so we quickly hid
the cases of Budweiser under the bushes in the
backyard. Then we each drank a warm one, and
somehow about that time I began to sober up a bit to
realize how crazy we had been. But after a few
minutes my friend said, "Come on, let's go clean
them out."

"What?" I said.

"Let's go back and get the rest of it," he said. Somehow he persuaded me to drive back with him down the same alley and go in and start unloading more cases of Budweiser. We were so stupidly drunk we thought they would ignore the missing beer from our first visit. Of course they *had* missed it; they had called the cops and the cops were in front of and inside the bar when we returned. But we never saw them. Next thing, I was back in the storeroom hefting two cases out the door when somebody came around the corner and screamed, "They're back!"

Heaving the case at him, I flew out the door and down the alley—right past my car, motioning my friend to follow. Two men never ran faster. I headed for a field, my friend for backyards and hedges. I caught a glimpse of him flying over the sidewalk, his legs pumping, his feet treading air. Meanwhile I hit the brush: I ran over large saplings and felt them pass between my legs; I plowed through briars and broke through fences. Then I lay with my face in the dirt and listened to the sirens. That afternoon I was a lifeguard; now, I thought, I am a hunted criminal.

An hour later, we had crawled home. Sober, scared, and desperate now because they had my car, we decided to take a gamble. First we called some friends at a party and got them to make up an alibi for us if it was needed. They would all swear we were with them all night. They would also tell of the two tough guys who crashed the party and then left in a hurry. *Then we called the police station and reported a stolen car.*

We said two tough guys had crashed the party and

left early. When we went outside, our car was gone.
The officer listening to this just said, "You boys
better get right down to the station house."

We cleaned up, sobered up, and dressed up in
preppy clothes and walked down the police station.
We doubted the bluff would work, feeling sure they
would just book us when we got down there. When
our parents heard, it would be all over. Both of our
fathers were lawyers, but we were beyond help now.
We walked into the station and up to the front desk.
The policeman behind the desk looked down at us
like he knew we were crawling in the dirt an hour
ago. I still felt sort of drunk and sort of panicky and
the whole incident began to look like a dream.

"So," he said, "I'll bet you college kinds think we
country policeman are pretty slow and stupid, eh?"

"Oh, no," I said while my knees started shaking.

"Oh, yes, you do," he said. "But let me tell you
something. You had your car stolen about two hours
ago, right? Well, we have already located your car
and it's in fine shape. You see, two hoods were trying
to rob a downtown bar. We came in, broke it up and
recovered your car. You boys just step outside and
get in the squad car. Officer Bass will take you to
the car."

I kept thinking this was their idea of a sick prank,
that any second Officer Bass would slap the cuffs on
and book me, but instead he simply drove us down
the street to the bar we had just plundered. He
didn't even make us go before the owners of the bar,
but it had been too dark and crowded anyway for
them to get a good look at us. When we went in, we

looked like grubby beach bums; now we looked like we stepped out of the L.L. Bean summer catalogue.

As he pulled up alongside the alley, Bass said, "There's your car, boys. Pretty nice work, eh?"

"Yeah, officer, you sure work fast. Did you catch the guys who stole our car and pulled this job?" my friend asked.

Officer Bass turned in the squad car and looked suddenly at both of us and smiled, "We didn't have to catch 'em, boys, because we know who they are, and we can just reel them in when we need them."

I almost fainted, but since we were out of the squad car we just waved and said thanks and got in the VW and drove away. That was our last robbery. Today we are both respected attorneys and one of us is in politics. The police must have been bluffing because they never bothered us again.

6

MILLIONAIRE'S ROW
Women Remembering

I N RESEARCHING FOR THIS BOOK, I sought out as many women as possible. In my younger days, I found it difficult to set up and conduct interviews with women, especially elderly women. Not only were they reluctant to open up to a stranger—a male—but I was too young. They did not understand my motive for interviewing them. Indeed, I was not always so interested in listening to women. Storytelling has sometimes been assumed to be a man's province, but I have found that women informants have at least as much to say as men and can tell stories just as well. However, they want to tell them to someone they know will understand.

Now that I have grown children and lots of gray hair, and have lived in north-central Pennsylvania for many years, I am more successful. Moreover, I have grown to appreciate women's stories more. As a younger man I was more interested in the frontier hunting and fishing stories that men like to tell. Women don't tell many hunting yarns, but they tell other kinds of stories that give a detailed and personal picture of the world they lived in years ago.

Once I locate a good female storyteller, my problem is keeping up with her. My women informants have a host of things to say—things that need to be said. Unlike many of the men, they didn't care who was going to read it. The women I talked to didn't hold back or worry about appearances or what the neighbors might think. An elderly woman speaks her mind.

These women have a sharp memory for details. They remember little events, particular scenes, and specifics like the weather, people's moods, the colors

154

and shapes of objects. More than texture, their narratives have a continuity, a sense of time unfolding, and a sense of place. Women's stories emphasize a woman's relationship to the world, her community, and her family.

Some of my informants, like Betty Orshaw, Catherine Voce, and Pauline Holcombe grew up in the northern part of Pennsylvania in tiny rural hamlets or, as in Catherine's case, in the wilderness. Because they were so isolated, they did not face the rapid social and technological changes brought on by the railroads after 1850—except perhaps in Pauline Holcombe's Dushore, where the railroad ran daily. From these women we get a rich mosaic of Pennsylvania's rural and small-town life in the early twentieth century.

Other women I interviewed have seen dramatic changes in their time. Lola Spangle of Williamsport moved to the city from a tiny town in Potter County because of the sudden affluence of a father, a timber merchant. She recalls some of the glitz and splendor of the days when lumber-rich Williamsport boasted more millionaires than any other small city in the United States.

Pauline Holcombe, who lives in a bright yellow Victorian home on Railroad Street looking down on the small town of Dushore, still keeps so busy that she hardly had time to see me. At eighty-five she bakes, sews, lays up jams, goes shopping at the Lycoming Mall, and remembers just about everything she needs to. She conducted her own interview, in a sense, by just beginning, "I'll begin at the beginning so you don't miss anything, and then I'll work up to my own family."

Edith Kahler now lives in Lock Haven, but grew
up on the mountain, way up the Coudersport Pike in
Caldwell. She chatted with me for two hours about
her life before the First World War. Her days had
been filled with hard work, but she was fortified by
an Appalachian stoicism. To her it had all been
good, all worth living, and she had no regrets and
recalled much happiness.

Up in Roaring Branch on Route 14, I visited
Catherine Voce in her limestone house
overshadowed by massive sumacs. Now in her
seventies, she keeps a loaded gun beside the door for
woodchucks. Catherine told me her entire life story,
vividly describing her adventures as a mountain
homesteader up on Rock Run in the 1930s. She feels
a certain nostalgia about her frontier days; they took
on a heroic aura as she told me about them. When
she is lonely, she cheers herself up by hunting
woodchucks. She demonstrated for me. That was
how our interview ended, with me crouching behind
her as she crept through the milkweed and under the
apple trees, poised for a shot at a woodchuck.

I found Mahalia Packer, a ninety-pound
grandmother, in Salona, a town just inside the
Nittany Valley along Fishing Creek. She gave me a
piercing look as she opened the door of her trailer,
located in her daughter's front yard. Halie's story
clearly shows the transition many people in Clinton
County made when they moved from the small
family farm to the factory or railroad town. In a
sense, Halie moved from the nineteenth century to
the twentieth, and she didn't like it. Her story
attests to the wave of state and federal projects that

swept over the region in this century. Halie's old farm at Blanchard now lies under the lake created by the Blanchard Dam. Halie's account of women's experience never strayed from a strict definition of propriety regarding what could be discussed. When I asked her about superstitions concerning "women's things," or menstruation, she just looked at me, wide-eyed, and then shrieked, "What?!" I realized my mistake. "Nothing," I said, "nothing."

I also found good storytellers among younger women. Betty Orshaw grew up in an isolated rural farm community a few miles north of Camptown, the inspiration of Steven Foster's "Camptown Races." Betty plays mandolin and sings traditional songs in a distinctive Appalachian style. Perhaps this explains her fondness for her past. Although Betty was born in the 1930s, she spent her childhood in such an isolated area, with only rudimentary comforts, that her childhood memories harken back to an earlier time. From her we can imagine what rural life was life at the turn of the century.

In her eighties, Rebecca Gross seems to manage quite well for a woman who lost both her legs in a car accident over thirty years ago. She invited me to her beautiful home in the Dunsmore section of Lock Haven along the river, just above a lock on the old Susquehanna Canal. She led an exceptional life, and once was the subject of a big spread in *Life* magazine.

Edith Casky was nervous about my visit. Although her daughter had recommended her as a good storyteller and although I had telephoned her to explain why I wanted to interview her, she didn't seem to like my looks when she glimpsed me over

157

her door chain. It did seem a little absurd for a moment: here I stood, a stranger, asking an eighty-year-old woman to let me in her house so she could tell me all about her childhood. I felt sorry for both of us. Finally, her sister persuaded her to open up. The interview progressed badly at first. Edith had recently suffered a stroke and felt she could remember almost nothing. Gradually, though—and this is always the fun of my project collecting life stories—I could see her memories float back bit by bit. Finally she quite happily retrieved some wonderful images. My favorite image in this book is that of the two young Swedish girls from Mountain Glen on their way to school walking through the engine works beside giant sooty locomotives and machines hanging in the dark.

Millionaires' Row
Lola Spangle, Williamsport

My father, Brooks Reese, was born on a poor farm in Port Matilda in Centre County. With twelve children and no money, the family could barely survive, so Brooks was apprenticed at age twelve to a sawmill run by the Miller family. Some say that by the age of sixteen Brooks Reese could estimate lumber better than anyone in Pennsylvania. By the age of seventeen, he hired on with one of the big lumbering companies up in Potter County. There he met and married my mother, a Lyman, whose ancestors had settled Potter County. I was born in

Austin in 1899, and a few years later the family moved to Williamsport. Over the next decade they had five more children.

My father's reputation as a lumber grader got him a job with the George B. Brion Company, but soon he and E. B. Sheriff formed their own lumber grading and selling company. In 1905 we lived at 22 Washington Boulevard. My mother took me to see the colored people who lived on Erie Street. She had never seen colored people before and she was frightened when she saw them. A few years later we moved to 912 Cherry Street. We went to the Valamont School and later to Williamsport High School on West Third Street.

I can recall the pleasures of being a teenager back then: things were simpler, we had more respect for each other, and the rich, the middle class, and not so well-off all mingled together. In the summer we rode to Indian Park in Montoursville, or River Park at Sylvan Dell to swim, canoe, or picnic. Sunday evenings we cruised on the old Hiawatha—a real paddle wheeler. On summer evenings we rode the open trolley cars to Valamont Park at the end of Woodmont Avenue to see the summer theatre. Our boyfriends—of course we had boyfriends—walked us to the movies at the Park Theatre and the Hippodrome. We would walk everywhere. In winter we skated on the river and sledded on the hills. The West Branch of the Susquehanna froze so thick we skated from Williamsport to Jersey Shore and back. Winter was colder then. Music filled our days, since most of us studied piano or violin or flute. Williamsport was a grand town with trolleys running everywhere; the new electric cars glided along West Third and Fourth

Streets, and all the big millionaires' houses brimmed with flowers, fresh paint, and happy people dancing in brightly lit ballrooms.

Millionaires' Row fired my imagination as a young girl. The great houses rose up from plots too small; their gables and cornices and dormers poked above the maples, bent and curved, jutted out into the sky, rose up and fell, and no two looked the same. How many people did it take to fill up one of those great mansions? My mother told me my father dreamed of living in one. She said one night when they still lived in Austin he returned from a trip to Williamsport and said, "You know, dear, when I walk along West Fourth Street and I look at those beautiful houses I dream that one day we will live there."

In my junior year of high school, we really did move into a run-down mansion my father was refurbishing— the E. R. Payne home at 1154 West Fourth Street. We were told Payne was Williamsport's first millionaire and thought the big house must once have been splendid. My father spent over thirty thousand dollars to refurbish the house, and when the workmen were done, it was a marvel. Seventeen-foot-high ceilings, great rugs for every room, crystal chandeliers, cherry and oak furniture, banisters carved and fitted in France, and even a few servants.

And a tennis court in the backyard that was never empty except in winter. When he turned forty, my father developed a passion for tennis. First he learned to play and then taught my brothers Brooks and Bob, who became quite good. At that time, tennis was a snob game. Tennis at the two or three other courts in town was by invitation only, but our clay court was open to everyone. I remember father stringing rackets and even buying sneakers for neighborhood kids. He was the first person to make tennis a popular sport in Williamsport, and later he helped found the Williamsport Tennis Club at Lymehurst. Once a year the sound of tennis balls would give way to the click of the city marbles tournament held on the netless tennis court. Today, a gas station stands on the corner where once our house stood.

Like many a Williamsport millionaire, my father's fortune rose, fell, and eventually collapsed. As World War I ended, the company found itself with millions of board feet of lumber on freight trains all over the country. The government orders were suddenly canceled. I know my father lost a fortune, made it back, and then lost it again. We came to regard that as normal in Williamsport. By this time, I was a young woman and I soon found myself engaged to Lyle Spangle whose father ran the freight office for the Pennsylvania Railroad.

Lyle survived the German U-Boat torpedoing of his ship, the *President Lincoln,* in World I. He spent many hours in the freezing Atlantic before a rescue ship plucked him out. Our married life together was happy. He worked in state and county offices while I stayed home and raised a family. We lived in a double house on West Third. Then a housewife had to bake, do laundry by hand, iron, cook, shop, and clean. Homemaking was a full-time job and I liked it. When women had their babies back then, they went to Williamsport hospital where they stayed for two weeks. None of this in-and-out like they have today. You had your own room and a crib right next to you. Nobody thought about birth control back then, by the way.

Socially, Williamsport offered everything. We attended dances, Mason functions, concerts, neighborhood picnics, and a host of other activities. Then, as now, Williamsport encouraged community involvement. We felt like we belonged to something. The years passed happily, our son and daughter grew up, and our boy graduated from Annapolis right after the Second War. Over the next four years, he became a navy pilot. When MacArthur invaded Korea at Inchon, my son volunteered to fly doctors and nurses in on an emergency mission. After refueling at one of the islands in the Pacific, the old transport they were flying suddenly exploded, killing everyone on board. Into a life as long and happy as mine, tragedy had to come sometime.

My daughter-in-law has remained close, and I see the children frequently. I'm still driving—I don't want to be around when I can't drive. My brothers Brooks and Bob still run the family lumber business and I live alone in these nice low-rent apartments for the elderly.

Life in Dushore
Pauline Holcomb, Dushore

Dushore was settled by shrewd and thrifty Germans and Irish in the early nineteenth century. They came here because they were land hungry. They were willing to clear off the rugged mountaintops, roll the logs and stumps down the sidehills, and plow the upland meadows of Sullivan County. They were smart and they were ambitious. In this harsh hill country, people just couldn't make it without brains and drive. By the 1860s the anthracite mines opened up in Estella and Bernice and provided plenty of employment for over thirty years. Logging was good up to the end of the First World War, and so were the two tanneries. The years between roughly 1835 and 1935 were the era of the small farm. Families made a good living with a few cows, sheep, turkeys, several acres of potatoes and corn, apple orchards, chickens, pigs, ducks, geese, and game from the woods. There was always so much to eat on a farm—even during the Depression. Several men made fortunes buying up produce around Dushore and selling it out of the area. This was a place to be if you were energetic and thoughtful.

My father grew up in Bradford County and attended the Elmira Business School around 1890. His schoolmate at the time was a Mr. Watson who later founded and became president of the IBM company. Father returned to Dushore where he worked as a mechanic and a bookkeeper. I remember him telling me about the township supervisor then: he could neither read nor write, but instead kept everything in his head and never forgot a transaction or a payment.

For a while my father repaired bicycles; then he worked in a factory making metal milk containers. In this shop they had five tinsmiths making over one hundred cans a week. My father lived in a

163

boardinghouse then. They liked to play various pranks on each other, too—like taking an old pail and covering it with frosting and red sugar flowers and sticking candles in the icing and serving it as a birthday cake, or putting a goat, cows, and pigs up in a man's room in the boardinghouse.

Dad was making fifteen dollars a week in 1903 working for Sam Coles, but he wanted more, and he told Sam he was going to quit if he didn't get a raise. That same day he rented a rig to take my mother— course, they weren't married yet—for a ride in the country. Well, they headed out the old turnpike toward Bernice when they heard the sirens from the iron foundry go off, so, being the loyal volunteer firefighter he was, he turned the buggy around and headed back into town. He got there just in time to see Sam Cole's store in flames. Now, Sam had the only plate glass window in town, and a volunteer was about to pitch something right through it when Dad stopped him and got them to put the fire out without wrecking the place. A few days later Dad got a raise. In a year Dad had saved two hundred dollars to buy a furniture store.

Of Eaglesmere I have many memories: of the rich Quakers from Philadelphia, of the Lakeside and Crestmont hotels. The place was so grand then. Sometimes, while visiting friends at the Lakeside Hotel, I would watch the rich arrive with their trunks, tennis rackets, and golf clubs. They would stay and stay all summer long. Lakeside had eighteen rooms, and on hot summer nights they'd open the doors and drop wispy cotton curtains over the entrances to get cross-ventilation. In the big homes

in Eaglesmere, the third floor was all set up for
recreation on rainy days. They could play pool or
shuffleboard or dance.

My earliest Eaglesmere memory was of my first ride
in a car. The year was 1908 and I was five. My
father took me over in the wagon from Dushore and
left me with friends. Suddenly the man drove up in a
bright red automobile. It was called, I later learned,
a Red Brush Automobile and was topless, fitted with
brass, and followed by a dust plume wherever it
went. The woman wrapped me in a white linen
duster, topped with scarf and bonnet, and away we
shot, flying over dirt roads at the maniacal speed of
twenty-five miles an hour. My first big thrill. When I
finally got home, I excitedly told everyone of my
adventure. My little brothers and sisters—for I was
the oldest—listened wide-eyed and then began to
bawl because they had not been there.

My father added an undertaker's business to the
furniture business. Back then, the two trades often
went together because the furniture stores provided
the caskets. Instead of just icing corpses down, my
father learned how to embalm. Draining blood from
the dead, according to the locals of the day, was the
devil's own work, but soon the practice became
standard. I would work in the furniture store during
my school years from 7:00 to 9:00 P.M. I'd listen to
Chopin, Beethoven, and Strauss on the gramophone.
Once my brothers took one of what they called the
rough coffins—the crates the coffins came in—and
hoisted Goofie Miller, who was dead drunk, into it.
They nailed the lid on and placed the crate in the
middle of town with flowers on the coffin. When he

165

awoke, he started screaming and kicked his way through the crate. Meanwhile all the onlookers panicked and ran up Railroad Street.

With the First World War came the great influenza epidemic. Fortunately, we had fine doctors in Dushore who pulled most of us through. In Dunshore the flu did not kill the elderly; instead, strong, vigorous young men grew feverish, developed pneumonia, and died—lots of them. I got it too. I recall standing in the store feeling fine one minute, then getting very dizzy, staggering home, and collapsing with a fever that ran high for five days. No vomiting, no diarrhea.

News of the Armistice came to Dushore by telegraph at the Pennsylvania Railroad station. The town went wild. My brother and I were minding the store when we heard about the big parade. The entire town would dress up and march over to Bernice. So we locked up the store, raced up to the barn, and tried to hitch up my father's team of black horses, Page and Harry. When they weren't pulling the hearse, they were delivering furniture. Only we couldn't harness them up until Bert Henry helped us, and soon we were on our way. I was fifteen, my brother, Pierson, was eleven. I couldn't control those frisky horses. We had mounted a great American flag in the whip-socket which flapped into the horses' hind ends and agitated them. The team trotted through town and out a country road—the opposite direction of the parade. Then the horses just went for a long country gambol, stopping to graze whenever they pleased, heading home only when their evening feeding time came. So we missed the

Armistice Parade. My mother told me as the parade
entered Bernice, the Dushore women placed scarfs
and kerchiefs over their faces because the influenza
had been bad there. This made the people of Bernice
so angry that for months they refused to shop in
Dushore.

My school years were memorable. By the time I
was a senior, we had only twelve in our class—and
only two were boys. Many had dropped out to take
good-paying jobs in the silk mills or mines because
their family needed their income. We played girl's
basketball, and we also saved for a class trip to
Washington, which we got, I recall summers on Lake
Makoma, outside LaPorte, how we would swim in
the dark water. Father bought a canoe called *Rosie
Jane* after my mother and made us swear never to call
it a canoe because Mother was afraid of canoes. I
recall floating on summer evenings far out on the
lake with my brothers playing the Victrola in the
canoe and singing along with the music. Everyone
sang so much then. Then at night the dances. And
beyond our cabin I can remember the ice-cutters in
winter, forty men working in crews cutting blocks of
ice, shaving, skidding, sledding the blocks into a
long warehouse beside the train station to be shipped
by the trainload to Wilkes-Barre and Scranton for
iceboxes all summer long.

On a busy business day in Dushore, the
drummers—traveling salesmen—came down from
the railroad station in rented carriages with their
goods in crates or suitcases. Farmers and wives
poured in from the country with eggs, butter, squash,
maple syrup, turnips, honey, knitted socks, and

potatoes to sell and trade for cloth, flour, coffee, and clothing. A man's suit was seven dollars when I was in school, and Dushore was a busy, bustling town where a man or a woman could make a good living.

Now that I'm eighty-five, I just want to keep going so I don't miss anything. I have so many things going on I just can't keep up with myself. I take pictures and do slide presentations of wildflowers when I'm not making jellies and jams or sewing clothes for people. Tomorrow I'm off to Woolrich to visit my nephew, Dick Holcomb, a vice-president in the company. I can hardly wait to get into that Woolrich outlet store.

Mountain Farm at Caldwell
Edith Kahler, Lock Haven

W hen my grandfather settled up here in 1860, they called it Mountain Spring, but today we call it Caldwell. I was born up on Grindstone Mountain in 1905, near where my son Malcolm lives today. I remember when they cleared the two hundred acres up there by pulling out the old stumps. They used the stumps for fences and they lasted a long time.

Around the time of the First World War, I attended a one-room schoolhouse. We took a shortcut to school that was two miles long. When the big snows came, father would hitch up one of the horses and attach a log chain to the harness and then to a log. He would ride along the path to school making a trench in the snow for us to follow. Often we couldn't see over the edge of the snow. Sometimes we were snowbound for a whole week. We didn't pay it any mind, though, because we had everything we needed. One time the snow lay over forty-eight inches deep.

My parents farmed, so they would "tend market," as they said, in Lock Haven once a week except during the coldest months. Potatoes grew fine up on the mountain, so that was our big crop. We could keep them in our cold cellar until spring. If they started sprouting, then we'd be sent down to rub the sprouts off. Some kinds of apples would keep all winter, too, if you treated them right. My mother canned over one thousand quarts a year and we helped her. There were eleven of us, with two sets of twins—all born at home in the parlor without a doctor, all healthy except my one brother. Mother died at the age of sixty-five, a happy but worn-out woman.

Mother made everything we wore, even our underclothes. The first store-bought coat I ever owned I got by picking huckleberries at five cents a quart. Lord, I picked a million berries to earn that coat. It was green, made out of a kind of plush, and it had an imitation fur collar. Coming down from the mountain into Lock Haven, you needed a good coat in winter. Mother and Father used to put a lantern in the wagon at their feet. Sometimes they would wrap newspapers across their chests to keep the wind out.

In summer Mother gathered all kinds of herbs to dry in the attic. She made herbal medicine for

169

sickness and teas for colds, headaches, and fevers. Herbs like longweed, catnip, spearmint, nettle, and asafetida dried under our eaves. I remember having to wear asafetida around my neck as a child. It smelled awful. I can't tell you what those herbs cured.

Father preserved pork by placing sections of the hog in a fifty-five-gallon barrel. Then he added salt and water until the brine was so thick an egg would float, leaving only a spot the size of a dime above the water. Then it was right. He would let the uncooked pork soak in the brine for six weeks. Then he would remove it and smoke it slowly over an apple wood or sassafras fire. I remember a strange hermit named Billy Brock who lived on the mountain. One time we saw this dirty and long-haired man go out to his brine barrel to get some pork. He reached in and pulled out a dead skunk. Then he turned to us, for he knew we were watching him, and said, "Huh, another one." Then he reached in and pulled out a piece of pork.

I left the mountain after what we called "country school" was over. I wanted to attend high school, so I had to come to live in Lock Haven. I was the first one from Caldwell to go to high school, and I had to work in the silk mill to pay my board.

Soon after I graduated from high school, I got married and set up housekeeping in town. I quit work and had two children during the first two years of marriage. That's all I had. My mother had eleven and didn't think anything of it, but the women of my generation who moved into town where the jobs were, they couldn't see the need for having a big family. Four children was a big family to those who lived in town.

My husband worked in the dye factory. When he was forty-six he had a fatal accident: while he was cleaning the dye out of one of the vats, the ventilation system shut off; suddenly he inhaled the toxic fumes and passed out. He died three days later. The doctors encouraged me to sue the company, but at first I was reluctant. Finally, I did and won three thousand dollars, which was a lot of money in those days. To support my children, I became a cook in a restaurant in downtown Lock Haven where I worked for nineteen years.

I don't think of any of it as hardship. It was a good life, a rich life, and my children and grandchildren are all doing well. My son lives up on the family land, and I live down here in Lock Haven where I am close to things.

Pine Creek Memories
Anne Wolfe, Slate Run

These towns along Pine Creek are really relics from the logging days. Gradually the schools began to close in the 1930s, so now all the kids are bused to Jersey Shore. Back in the 1920s, bobcats were still plentiful and the state paid a fifteen-dollar bounty on them. Today they are making a comeback and we see them from time to time.

The whiskey would flow on the Fourth of July when we had big dances and lots of good fiddlers.

The men would sneak out of the dance and hit the white mule they'd hide behind the bushes. The boys would sneak out and steal some, drink it. That's how they first tasted it. They smoked and chewed, too, when they were kids. Boys picked up lots of bad habits growing up around railroad men.

We bought the General Store here in Slate Run in 1946 and ran it for over thirty years. Billy hopped a freight to ride to Jersey Shore to get a loan. We worked so hard and didn't take a vacation for twelve years, but when we did, our neighbors begrudged us the vacation. They'd say, "Oh, it must be hard to come back to Slate Run after seeing all those fancy places. Is the price of bread going up?" We just had to grin and take it, because in such a small place your neighbors know everything.

Bill worked up in the stone quarry while I tended store. It was lonely sometimes. Then he worked on the highway.

We kept things simple in the store, catering to a small but steady group of customers. Sometimes we got paid and sometimes we didn't. One time a man owed us over a thousand dollars, and he just wouldn't pay. The bank said I had to sheriff him out, like it or not, so we got the sheriff and they sold his property because he owed back taxes, too. Lord, we hated to do it.

During the smallpox epidemic around 1920, the doctor came down from Blackwell and gave us all inoculations. It was a bad batch, and we all got very sick. My arm swelled up and Doc White sent my sister down to Jersey Shore on the train because she had lockjaw. Next day she came back in a

coffin. I was only four but I can remember it.
Midwives Idy Coleman and Emma Swagert washed
her and laid her out at home. The casket was a
rough box. After the viewing, we went to the
church for the funeral and they buried her
up there.

Homesteading in Rock Run in the 1930s
Catherine Voce, Roaring Branch

My married name is Voce, pronounced "Vous,"
and my maiden name is Wismer, Pennsylvania
Dutch. I grew up in Franconia, a small town
between Souderton and Harleyville, above
Norristown. It was a Mennonite town where we
all spoke German. My father and uncles were
wheelwrights and tool sharpeners; later, when cars
came, his brothers worked on cars, but my father
would have nothing to do with the automobile.

Mennonites daresn't drink, but my father was a
drinking man. During Prohibition he was afraid to
drink the moonshine, so mother made wine for him.
"At least I'll know what he's drinking," she said. I
learned to make beer when I was eighteen, and it
was so good they called it the "fire extinguisher."

Growing up the way I did, without any medicine
or electric or car or gas and raising most of our own
food, made it easy for me to go homesteading
later on.

A few years after Charlie and I got married, we

came up to where Tioga and Lycoming and Bradford and Sullivan counties all come together—along Rock Run. We stayed in a cabin high up in the mountains, miles from any town. We liked it so much we bought the place for three hundred dollars and moved up two weeks later. We knew we could live for a long time up there on the good Montgomery County money we had.

The first night there, we were sitting on the porch when Charlie heard a buzz. "That's a rattlesnake in the foundation," he said, and he put his gun in there and shot, and it stopped. We went back to Franconia right then and there, because there might be a den in the cellar. He came back a week later, tore down the whole thing, and rebuilt it. Charlie was a stonemason and could do just about anything.

Folks told us there was no rattlers on our mountain—the next mountain, yes—but then we learned the C.C.C. boys had disturbed a den and sent rattlers skittering all over the hills. I always wore high-laced leather boots up to my knees because of the snakes. I wore riding pants, a men's mackinaw shirt, and a tam on my head. Folks in town must have thought I looked strange, but I didn't care. I was young, in love, and happy on the mountain.

The cabin was up above Grover, near Ellenton, on the second branch of Rock Run. Once you got there, you were in. It didn't pay to work in town when you lived up there. Lord, I loved it. Sometimes, when the wind was right I could hear a cowbell from a distant farm. When the weather turned around we could hear the whistle of the S. and N.Y. go

Poop!—*Poop!*—*Poop!* "It's gonna snow," Charlie would say, And it did.

We lived up there for five years during the Great Depression. We'd go for weeks without going to town. Because I didn't want to go in, I'd stretch it out a week or more. I knew right down to the penny how much to spend. Prices didn't change then. Three pounds of coffee for ninety-two cents. Coffee, sugar, flour, and salt were all I needed. One year we spent just a hundred dollars. That was it.

We raised potatoes, vegetables, goats, chickens, and always had milk, cheese, cream, eggs, and venison. I'd can the venison. Of course, we had no electric or gas. I'd put meat and milk in a bucket and lower it into the well. That was my refrigerator.

The winter of 1936 was rough. Snow over the fences. Four feet high. We were snowbound for a month. I loved every minute of it. The fields had waves in them like the ocean, white and shining. I'd run the trap lines with Charlie and sometimes I'd go alone in snowshoes. One time I had to shoot two big coons in the traps along Rock Run with their big sad eyes looking at me. Then I had to lug them up a steep cliff covered with an ice-crust. Ugh! Charlie walked down to Leolyn to get the mail. Leolyn was nothing more than a post office. When he got back, he said, "You know, Catherine, they've got the snow all cleared off Route 14. Can you believe that?"

The snow stayed all winter, and so did we. We got fat on goats' milk and read the *Rural New Yorker* magazine, and other old magazines people gave us, by the light of the oil lamp. I played an old organ I bought for thirty dollars, and we made maple syrup.

The first year we made syrup was silly. What greenhorns we were. We bored big holes in ten trees and got about ten gallons. We boiled the sap for days, and it wouldn't turn. Finally we got about one pint of maple syrup. We used the wrong kind of trees and the wrong tap.

"What is the difference in these maple trees?" Charlie asked a neighbor.

"There's a difference. I just don't know what it is," the neighbor said.

Finally, Charlie learned from the C.C.C. boys that the maple with its branches up—the heart maple, they called it—is the good one, the sugar one. The soft maple has its branches down and you did not want that. Next year, I ran one hundred trees by myself because Charlie had to go to work. What a lot of work! Cutting the firewood with a bucksaw was the hardest part. We had nice, broad boiling pans, and we canned lots of syrup.

I had a forty-four-forty Winchester for hunting. A saddle gun with lever action it was. I still have it. I love to hunt, though now it's only rabbits, woodchucks, and porcupines. The first year I hunted up on Rock Run in the thirties, Charlie put me on stand and drove two buck past me. One was a nice big one and I shot at him. He jumped when I shot, so I followed him into the woods. Then I met another hunter who said, "I heard you shoot. You must have hit him because there's blood. Come on, let's follow the blood trail."

So we went away, and then I thought: here I am

176

following a strange man into the woods. I must be
crazy. "You can have the deer, mister, I'm going
back," I said. He found the deer down by Rock Run
and he brought it to us. He was a neighbor on the
next mountain.

My second hunting season wasn't much better. I
told Charlie I was going to hunt on a big flat rock up
on the ridge above the house. He and a friend were
going down Rock Run. "Don't shoot back at the
house; we might come back and you'll shoot us,"
Charlie said.

He was always telling me don't do this and don't
do that. It was freezing out on that rock, but I knew
the deer crossed there. Soon I heard shots from the
field. Then two buck come right across me. I wait
till they clear the house and then I start shooting.
Every time I shoot, the big buck jumps. I shoot, he
jumps. I must be shooting under him. The little buck
comes right up to me. Squiggly horns. He looks.
Now, I've got buck fever. I can't shoot at all. Oh,
was I feeling stupid.

The next year was different. Charlie got one the
first day, and the morning of the second day was
thick fog. "I'm going down to the spring to hunt. I
know something will come through there," I said.

"It's too foggy, you'll get yourself killed," Charlie
said.

"Naw, they can't even see me, I said.

So I went on down to the spring and sat. I was
listening to a squirrel when I saw the outline of a
huge buck come around the hillside. He came
toward the spring. I up and shot, and you know

177

what? He made one big leap. Oh, I couldn't have missed him. I had it right on his heart. I heard him crashing, and I went down and he was in the pin cherries lying down, you know, and trying to move his front legs like this, trying to get up and run. Charlie always said, "You get a deer down, you keep shooting," so I shot him in the neck and that was the end of it.

Charlie heard the shots and came running. When he saw the deer, he said, "You would have to kill such a big one. I seen that deer before. He's a Michigan deer by the size of him. Long snout, gray coat. Well, just don't stand there, gut him."

"Ain't you going to help me?" I asked.

"It's your deer," Charlie said.

I think he was a little jealous, but he finally gutted the deer and slung him to a pole, but I couldn't hold up my end, he was so heavy. He tanned that hide using the brains and made a pack-sack for his traps. "Mr. Boone," I called him.

We moved down into Roaring Branch here after that. Lived in the little farmhouse across the road there that they later made into the Wheel Inn. Charlie worked for Mr. Case in Canton as a stonemason. We'd go to the movies at the Rialto Theater in Canton two or three times a week. Then we built this house ourselves right smack up against the mountain here. I helped him lay the stones. He died in 1972 of a stroke. Then I had a friend, Fred, lived with me for seven years. He was a good man and took me all over the place. Then he died in 1982. There was no point in getting married this old. I'm eighty-two. I'm lonely now, especially on weekends when my friends are doing things with their husbands.

If I were young again and had wings to fly, I'd fly back up on the mountain above Rock Run and live in our cabin. When you're young and in love, it makes all the difference. All I heard were the birds, a distant cowbell, and sometimes the S. and N.Y. whistle when the wind was right. I was in love and I was happy.

That's enough talk. Let's go outside and stretch a bit. I'll show you my garden. Maybe I can get that other woodchuck that's eating me out of house and home. Hand me that four-ten over there, and watch out, 'cause it's loaded.

Now, here's where Mr. Coon comes for his cat food every night. I ought to shoot him, but I just can't. He's so big. Sits here outside the screen door and licks his paws and goes, "Mmm yum, yum, yum." Lately he gets here early, or Mr. Possum will beat him out. Quarter to nine. Now this is my sweet apple tree. The porcupines love sweet apples. Two years ago I killed so many I stopped counting. Maybe seventeen. They come off the mountain and wake me up at night with their weird sounds. Did you ever hear them? It's a "Wee-wee-yum-yum-yee-yee-mum-mum" noise, like that, and I don't like it. So I get up in the night with my .410 and my flashlight and shoot them. One night I got six. I buried them behind the barn in the soft soil. No, I don't like porcupines. Come on. Keep low and quiet and maybe we can get a shot at Mr. Woodchuck.

It's so overgrown around my garden, I can't keep up. These are currants, asparagus, potatoes, garlic, and tomatoes. Now, look inside that pen. Just look at that lettuce. Oh! He's eating me out of house and home. I put boards up and he goes right under—look at that. Watch out—I've got a muskrat trap over there. One way or another, I'll get him. That? Oh, that's just a big black snake. Leave him. He's OK. Here, take some garlic home with you.

Farm Woman
Mahalia Packer, Salona

My name is Mahalia Packer, but my children and grandchildren and friends all call me Halie. I only weigh about ninety pounds and I'm eighty-one years old, but I gave birth to ten children, and nine are still living. All my life I worked hard, and when I was young I did the work of a man.

I was born on a farm right near where the Howard Dam is along Bald Eagle Creek. That was right around the beginning of this century. My family's name was Holt—German. My grandmother was part Indian.

My mother had twelve children and ten lived. Growing up on a farm was the best thing in the world, but we worked hard all the time. Farm people had to "go it" if they wanted to make a living. You couldn't loaf. You had chores as soon as you could walk. We'd stand on chairs at the sink to do the dishes. We'd trot along behind the men cutting wheat and tie up the sheaves. We'd carry and carry

buckets of water until our arms were ready to fall off.
Washday meant lots of water and lots of scrubbing.
And women want to get in shape today. Ha!
Washing would make what they call "working out"
look easy. Yep. We worked night and day, but still it
was a good life.

Nowadays the girls are always changing their
clothes. Back then, we wore the same dress for three
days—with a clean apron every day.

We didn't work on Sunday. "If you work on
Sunday the Lord will put you in the moon," they
said.

There were always good things to eat on the farm.
My mother always was cooking. We'd help make
scrapple, liverwurst, cracklings, lard, *ponhaus,* and
hams when they killed a hog. We ate much more
pork than beef on the farm. We hardly ever ate
game. My father used to set nets in the Bald Eagle
Creek for fish. Now he daresn't do this, 'cause it was
against the new fish rules, but he did it anyhow and
caught lots of fish.

We made our own birch beer and our own herb
teas out of catnip, sassafras, pennyroyal, and
hemlock. You didn't see a doctor for every ache and
pain. You doctored yourself up. I never saw a doctor
until I moved to Lock Haven and had my first child.

Women and men were equal on the farm. My
father and mother had an equal say about
everything. The only thing a woman couldn't do was
plow by hand. But if you were a woman you were
needed so much on the farm that you had to stop
going to school by the eighth or ninth grade. I could
have gone to college; Lord knows, I don't lack the

brains. But I was held back because I was needed.

I wish my children had grown up on the farm. It's such a wonderful place. There was the spring house. It's a stone building with spring water running through it, usually in a stone trough around the edges. It's like a refrigerator. Cool in summer. You can keep raw milk in there for days. I always felt special about that.

For entertainment, we all played a musical instrument on the farm. We played the organ, piano, accordion, and of course we sang.

Now, when I got married I moved to Lock Haven because my husband worked on the railroad. The railroad employed many people back then. I never really liked living in town.

Now, we had ten children. Don't ask me why we had so many. I loved every one of them dearly then as I do now, but ten children is a lot of kids. Fact is, we didn't give it much thought. The Bible said, "Multiply," and boy, did we multiply. I had seven girls and two boys who lived.

> They tramp on your lap when they're little,
> And they tramp on your heart when they're big.

Today women have a better life. They can choose more what they do, and they don't have the big families we did then. All I ever knew was hard work. The farm was and still is the best place to grow up, but in many ways it doesn't prepare you for the world. You're too isolated.

My children and grandchildren and great-grandchildren come to see me all the time now.

They live around here. I tell them just what I think, but I try not to tell them what to do. "If you make a mistake, you're not going to blame it on me," I say.

What advice do I have for people? Lord, I don't know. I know I'm not scared of dying, because I'm ready. Facing eternity without the Lord—that would really frighten me. Live a good Christian life. Don't be afraid of hard work. Stay young by keeping busy. That's it.

A Bradford County Childhood
Betty Orshaw, Milan

I was born in 1930 over in LeRaysville. I'm fifty-six. We lived three miles out of town on a two-hundred-acre dairy farm. LeRaysville is in northern central Pennsylvania. The closest city is Binghamton, New York. Scranton is almost an hour away to the south. North of Towanda and the Susquehanna River, it's just tiny towns and isolated farms all the way to the New York State line.

My mother and father had seven children—six girls and one boy. My grandfather lived with us after my grandmother died. That was common in those days, having a grandparent live with you.

We had no electricity until the 1940s. I was a teenager when we got an electric light bulb in the front room. That was it, one naked bulb hanging from a cord. We had some sort of battery that had to be charged every few days by a gas engine. We finally got public electricity in 1953 when other folks were getting their television sets.

Our water came from a spring a few hundred yards from the house. We had no pump. It seems I spent my youth carrying water and splitting wood. Of course, there were many of us, and these chores were often more like play than work. We were poor, but we didn't know it; we worked hard, but we didn't notice.

Early in the morning, my father worked the farm. During the day he would walk three miles to the sawmill where he would work for eight hours, and then he would come home and do the chores.

I remember Christmas the best. Each one of us would get one toy. We all thought we were the luckiest children in the world. Sometimes it was something Mother had made, and sometimes it was boughten with money sent by my aunt in Binghamton. If you got a doll, you were really lucky. You would have that doll for the rest of your life. The older kids would get long underwear and long stockings because Mother was afraid we might freeze to death. She dressed us warm. Then, in our stockings hung by the mantel, we would get a few nuts and an orange. That was it, except for the big dinner.

The night before Christmas, we were all excited, and usually we girls would all get into one bed and listen to Mom and Dad downstairs popping popcorn and making fudge, and it smelled real good. We never got to sleep before midnight, and we were up before daylight.

Another event I remember was butchering the

hogs. We liked this because my grandfather would take the pigs' bladders and block off the ends and blow them up for us. They were our playground balls, and they held up to kicking and throwing for a long time. I remember we used to use the pigs' tails to grease the pan in the kitchen. Grandfather was also expert in whittling. He made us toys and tools out of wood. We also played checkers with him, and at night we would sit around the fire and play "Button, Button, Who's Got the Button?" or "I Spy." We would eat apples or cracked nuts. I remember putting a flatiron between my knees and breaking nuts with a hammer. Sometimes Grandfather would sing a song that went like this:

> Ke mo ki mo de ro ro
> Hi de ho rump dump dump
> Fiddle and a wink dum
> Nip cat tip cat sing song
> Polly won't you ki me O.

My grandfather had arthritis, so it was hard for him to get around. He used to take me fishing with him so I could help. We would ride in the horse and buggy to the pond. Sometimes he would bring his gun, and after he got tired of catching bass he would shoot woodchucks. We ate them, you see. I would be just like a dog when he shot one. I would run out across the field and I would lug the big old thing back to him. You have to cut out a gland under the arm for the woodchuck to taste good. Whistlepigs, we ate a lot of them. My dad had tuberculosis when he was in his late thirties, and I can remember the county health nurse coming to check on him. We had to boil all his dishes and wash all his clothes separate from ours.

I went to school in a one-room schoolhouse that had six grades. We had a water pail in school and we all drank from the same dipper. When it snowed, we went to school in the sleigh. I had to stop at the store once a week to get Redman chewing tobacco for my grandfather. It embarrassed me, but he gave me extra money for candy. When I was six, my younger sister was born. It was a chilly morning and we were sent outside to sit in the sun while the baby was coming. Then they called us in, and there was the baby lying on the opened oven door while a neighbor lady was washing it.

Music was important to my family, and it still is to me. I perform all over the area, mostly singing the old-time songs with my son, Mark. He knows all the old songs too. Lots of people like to hear them. They bring back the old days. Why, we sing a song called "Over the Hills to the Poorhouse" that brings tears to the old folks' eyes. You see, there was a county home—still is, in fact—a few miles from here in Burlington. Why, back in the Depression, lots of people went bust and had to live in the home. They called it the poorhouse. Anyway, my parents sang and played instruments, and I grew up playing and singing. To me, the most exciting thing I ever heard was "The Grand Ole Opry" on Channel 650. My brother brought a radio home and all we heard was static. Then suddenly it came through—Roy Acuff, Jimmy Rodgers, Kitty Wells. I wanted it to never end. Next, we got a record player and records. I was just crazy for the stuff. We still have all our old records. Then we started going to country dances in Stevensville. I was about fourteen when I first danced.

Bradford County has strong musical traditions, lots of good old fiddlers, like Harvey Wright, and guitar pickers. When I became a singer as a young girl, I got to know all of them. Sometimes I would sing on the radio and sometimes I would sing in church. I'm a shy person by nature, but when it comes to singing, well, I'm ready to go. That's when I let all my true feelings out.

Lady Editor
Rebecca Gross, Lock Haven

My ancestors sailed for America from Europe in 1724. Five years later, these Protestant Germans were working prosperous farms in Lancaster County, Pennsylvania. Within two generations, members of the Gross family had settled along the West Branch of the Susquehanna River. Whenever the colony signed a treaty or bought new land from the Indians, my relatives quickly settled in the new territory. My grandfather grew up in Montgomery and then went to Selinsgrove as an apprentice buggymaker. While there, he fell in love with Lydia Wagner, who agreed to marry him. But the Civil War had just started, so my grandfather enlisted and left to fight. When he returned four years later, Lydia was waiting; they married and bought a large

187

farm in Muncy where they lived happily for many years. They raised seven children on what we came to call the family homestead. Then one day my grandfather was told by state officials that he would have to sell the farm. He couldn't argue. The state purchased the land to build the Muncy Correctional Facility for Women. The last thing born on the old farm was a colt named Grover Cleveland. I grew up with that horse and rode him as a young girl. I would sit on him for hours.

My father went to the Muncy Normal School to become a teacher, but it didn't pay, so he got a job as a weighmaster with the Pennsylvania Railroad in Lock Haven. At this time, things were changing fast along the West Branch. As the logging began to play out, the corporations began prospecting in the mountains for iron ore, clay, and coal, and they found all three. So we lived amidst the rumble and clang of this busy railroad town.

One day during my senior year at Lock Haven High School—this was in 1922—I was called to the superintendent's office. Somewhat nervous, I was surprised when he asked if I was interested in a newspaper job with the new weekly paper in town. The editor had asked him to recommend a good journalism prospect, and he thought of me, since I was editor of the school magazine. "How much does it pay?" was my first response.

Of course, I was interested, and when the editor interviewed me and told me the job paid five dollars a week, I was thrilled. Five dollars a week to anybody whose weekly allowance was fifteen cents was untold wealth. So I went to work. That first week, I fell in love with the newspaper business. Although I planned to study journalism in college, I stayed with the weekly newspaper that first year, saving money and learning the business. The name of the paper was the *Clinton County Times.*

At the *Times* I did it all: I ran the press, loaded the paper, proofread, covered news stories, wrote them up, and set type by hand using the "case." The case was a large box divided into small compartments, each compartment filled with dozens of a certain letter like *a* or *e* or *g*. We'd hold the stick—the column-sized plate in our left hand—and pick the letters out with the right hand. It was a kind of typing, but infinitely slower. And I loved it all. I couldn't get enough of it.

The paper would come out on Saturday and the folks coming into market from the outlying towns would read it to find out now much to charge for their goods. By year's end, I had saved and borrowed enough money to attend Temple University in Philadelphia. At last I would go to a real journalism school.

For a year and a half I studied at Temple. Midway through my sophomore year of college, I returned home to Lock Haven for Christmas vacation. As soon as I got home, the editor of the *Lock Haven Express* asked me if I would work for him for a few weeks over the vacation. I said yes. The *Express* was a daily newspaper, and in no time the thrill of getting out the daily news was in my blood. The editor must have known I'd find it irresistible. When it came time for me to return to Temple, the editor asked me to stay on, and I said yes. I could finish college later. I worked for the *Express* for an entire year until another man offered me another opportunity.

On a cold December day in Lock Haven, State Senator George B. Stevenson stopped me on the street and asked me into his office. He said, "How would you like a scholarship to go back to college— only this time the University of Pennsylvania?"

You see, back in those days the state disbursed aid to students through state senators. Can you imagine the potential for favoritism and corruption that system had? That's why they soon did away with it. But back then the state senators distributed the wealth to whomever they wanted. Anyway, I accepted the scholarship and went to Penn. The professor of journalism there told me an internship would be best for me, so he arranged for me to work in the research department of the *Philadelphia Inquirer*. And that is where I spent a semester, working without pay but learning a great deal.

Next year, as I was finishing my studies at Penn, I was contacted by Mr. Reilly, who wanted to buy the *Lock Haven Express.* He said if I could come up with a third of the price of the paper I could be part owner and editor. After talking with my father and going to the bank for the loan I needed, I bought into the paper and became its editor. I was twenty-six. I was the only female editor in the state. That year, 1931, the Depression began to choke the country, but I felt I could survive as an editor. Because I had worked so hard before and gotten along so well, the people on the paper accepted me, teaching me what I needed to know. We put out a good paper.

Soon I started the Pennsylvania Woman's Press Association—an organization to promote women in journalism. We were accused of starting a union at first, and in a way we were; we quietly helped women move ahead in a profession dominated by men. Of course, I have to say men never held me back in journalism; they always sought me out to do the job—they needed me and I was ready. Women's pay was much lower, though.

So I ran the *Express* for many happy and successful years. Then suddenly I had a bad automobile accident which caused both my legs to be amputated. I was out for a year, not able to work, an invalid. But I came back. We built an elevator up to the second floor of the *Express* and eventually I got a car that I could manage through hand controls. I made some mistakes, but I carried on as editor from 1931 until 1970, when, at the age of sixty-five, I retired.

Of all the events I covered, none was worse than the flood of 1936. A heavy storm just sat over the area for three days, and it rained and rained and rained. Then nearly all of the town was flooded. The water was deep downtown. Thousands were "treed in their attics," as we said then. They had to deliver food by boat because they couldn't get all the people out. The army drove in tanks to rescue people and deliver food. I got a ride in one. The newspaper office was completely under water. But we felt we had to do something: we had to carry on, so we went up to the college, got a mimeo machine, and ran off a newspaper and distributed it by boat for free. We operated out of my living room. After that flood, I got deeply involved in flood control and helped start

191

the Flood Control Association—the impetus that
eventually got the dams built above Lock Haven and
Renovo on the West Branch.

I am eighty-three now. With two artificial legs I
still get around rather well, although I am reluctant
to drive. Until recently I sat on the board of a
number of organizations, and I work for free on
community functions as often as possible. We hear a
lot about women competing in the workforce today.
In my life I cannot say I have been held back by
men, nor have I found it difficult to compete with
them. If a woman knows her stuff and knows it well,
she will do all right.

Growing up Beside the Engine Shops
Edith Casky, Renovo

The great red brick buildings stand east of town;
the tracks still run up to the giant doors. Once,
during the height of the lumber-and-coal era in
north central Pennsylvania, the engine shops in
Renovo served thousands of locomotives and railroad
cars and cabooses running thousands of miles of
track. Growing up in Renovo made you feel like you
were at the center of things. Everything came here
to get fixed. We kept everything rolling. I can't tell
you what it is like to lose that feeling of economic
security, to lose it when you are young and never get
it back. That's what I want to talk about.

We grew up in a place called Mountain Glen, a
little hollow beside the engine shops. We called it

Smoky Corners because the smoke from the shops
filled the hollow. On the way to school, we could
take a shortcut through the shops. The shop bosses
didn't mind before the strike. After the strike, we
had to go a long way around. I can see my sister and
me walking through the dark rooms in our clean
dresses with the great greasy engines, big as chicken
coops, hanging from the beams in the ceiling. The
roof was forty feet high, the room bigger than a gym.
My heart beat faster, but we were never afraid
because the workmen would always say hello to us.

All of the twenty families in Mountain Glen were
Swedish. My father's family was named Arvidson and
my mother's family Suderberg. In the lumber camps
they changed Arvidson to Anderson. My grandfather
Arvidson came over from Sweden to work as a
blacksmith in the logging camps. He and his wife
had five boys and then she died. He had to place the
boys in a county home in Williamsport; in a few
years, he married again and the boys came to live
with him and his new wife. The oldest boys were
now fifteen and sixteen, so they went to work in the
lumber camps. That was the age when they started.

Grandfather Suderberg (my mother's side) also
came from Sweden to work in the logging business.
He left his wife and three children behind because
they couldn't afford to emigrate and because his wife
was taking care of her parents. After six years, she
came over, and husband and wife were reunited and
then had three more children.

So many Swedes lived in Renovo in the early
nineteen-hundreds that we had our own Swedish
Lutheran Church. The old folks used to speak

193

Swedish around the house, but during the First
World War they stopped because speaking a foreign
language was considered unpatriotic. We followed
Swedish customs, too. On Christmas Day we dined
on fish called lutefisk that was a kind of salt cod we
soaked for days. It was delicious, as was the sauce
made from the brine. We kept candles lit in every
window and had to run around making sure they
burned safely. This was before electricity. We burned
kerosene for light.

In those early days of the century, Renovo was
gay, prosperous, and bustling. We never felt isolated
because passenger trains rolled in and out of town
three times a day. Folks were coming from and going
to New York, Harrisburg, Philadelphia, and Buffalo.
You just hopped on a train. Renovo seems more
isolated today, especially to the elderly. We have to
drive thirty minutes through the woods and along
the river to get to Lock Haven. When I was a girl,
the town was prosperous—so prosperous with the
Pennsylvania Railroad shops we thought it couldn't
end. Then came the strike of 1922.

Looking back, it seems the reason for all those
trains, mainly the lumber and the coal industries,
were giving out, and some kind of change was about
to come. The men walked off the job when I was
fourteen years old. Everyone alive then (I am eighty
years old) remembers that day vividly because things
went downhill after the strike. It was like the Lock
Haven strike—the Hammermill or International
Paper strike: a long bitter struggle, often pitting
family against family, friend against friend. And, in
the end, the town is damaged. No one back then

thought the Pennsylvania Railroad engine shops would cut back. Railroading was the backbone of the country: trains loaded with logs, cut timber, coal, clay, food, new automobiles, bricks, and people rolled daily through our small mountain town. How could it ever end? At night we danced to orchestras and ate in fine restaurants; on Sunday we dressed in fine clothes and attended beautiful churches. The railroad paid good wages to everyone, and the foremen and shop bosses lived like the upper class.

My husband died seven years ago. He worked in the shops all of his life. When they offered him the chance to go back to work, he went back along with many others, causing bitterness among those who wanted to prolong the strike. Today Renovo is a shadow of its glory days. The elderly here live on their railroad pensions and the welfare people move into the low-income housing units.

7

SHOT FOR A WOODCHUCK
Men Remembering

THE MEN IN THIS CHAPTER RANGE in age from fifty to ninety-five years old. All have been vigorous achievers and have seen and accomplished much. The older men, like Charlie Simpson and John Youngmans, are venerable, even heroic, probably because they have endured life cheerfully for so long. Most of them were skeptical about being interviewed. What did they have to say? Yet during our hours together, so many images of their past lives came welling up that they struggled for the right words to describe the fields they had plowed, the women they had loved, the children they had raised, the tunes they had played, the winters they had weathered, the sicknesses they had survived, and the myriad changes they had seen. Most of these elderly gentlemen had lived through two-thirds of this century, and many will live to see the next.

These monologues, collected from conversations, form a picture of life in central Pennsylvania that spans many decades. On a local or regional scale, these stories describe constant social, economic, and technological change. Every decade since the French and Indian War has seen violent upheavals along the Susquehanna's West Branch. Indian raids, the Revolution, exploration into the interior, rafting, hunting, trapping, farming, canal and road building, logging, coal mining, the settlement of towns, the rise of small businesses, the railroads— every decade brought novelties and new problems. And many industries—coal and timber, and later dairy farming—came and went fast. Surprisingly, wars in Europe and troubles in the national economy had little effect on the region; even the Depression had a muted impact because of the natural bounty of the area and its relative isolation. Factories stayed open, and the Civil Conservation Corps brought public works projects to the area. Central Pennsylvanians did not lose their sense of self-sufficiency even during the nation's hardest times.

The line between a personal history and an embellished narrative, a yarn, is not always clear. The first brief story, "Shot for a Woodchuck," comes from Harry Clark of Collomsville in the Nippenose Valley, who may have stretched a point here and there. Even though the story's events happened over forty years ago, Harry was careful to avoid family names because they are still well known in the valley.

Most of my informants took their autobiographical task more seriously. Now in his nineties, still practicing law in Williamsport, John Youngmans told "The Flood on Antes Creek," "The Calico Dress," and "Runaway Recruit" with ease, as though he had been telling them for decades—which he probably has. He showed me a photograph of members of his extended family—nearly a hundred of them—taken at a family gathering at the cabin along Antes Creek.

Phil Marks's story about his father, a Jewish immigrant peddler in the lumber camps, also reaches back to the early part of the century. Continuing in his father's trade, Phil has run a clothing store in Renovo for almost half a century. Although I had visited Phil before, I never could sit him down long enough to hear him talk at length. When I met him by chance on the street in November 1988, he took me into his store, made me comfortable, and began pouring out his family history. I had no recorder, so I wrote fast.

Another teller who calls up the past is Veris Metzger, a hermit farmer who seems to have stepped out of a Civil War movie. Veris lives alone on his mountain farm off the road from Jersey Shore to Wellsboro, up on Joe's Run. His reminiscence ends with a vestigial witty anecdote. The "Mountain Fiddler" is Harvey Wright who now lives just over the New York State line. An amazing musician at eighty, Wright belongs to the tradition that produced Jehile Kerkoff of Susquehanna County. I visited the old man in his house hung over a cliff with Mark Orshaw, a student of mine, and Mark's father, a relative of Harvey's. The old fiddler played for two twenty-five-minute sessions with Mark back-timing on the guitar and me frailing the five-string. Harvey had a mind as clear as his fiddle notes.

Another well-known fiddler, Harry D'Addario of New Berlin, attained almost celebrity status before the radio and phonograph cut into the live music tradition. The good people of Union and Snyder counties needed young Harry to play for dances, frolics, and ice-cream socials. Well into his seventies, Harry still fixes and sells violins. I had visited Harry a number of times, marveling at his impressive collection of fiddles, before I heard his story.

Now in his nineties, Charlie Simpson has worked his "Nesbit Farm"—now right next to a modern elementary school—for over sixty-five years. The rich, flat land has yielded good crops since the first plow turned it before the Revolution. We talked as we strolled over his property—it seems a good life to live on a productive farm in such beautiful surroundings.

As I began to talk to the Pfirmans in their home, I was doubtful about the interview. Both husband and wife were quiet, almost withdrawn, perhaps in poor health. I considered ending the interview. However, as we began to talk, Mr. Pfirman began to recall days of action and adventure. The trains touched everyone in his youth: boys dreamed of trains and learned how to hop slow freights to Lock Haven and Williamsport. But God help you if you had to jump from a fast-moving train.

People in Nesbit warned me that Louis Stanley was religious and would start preaching at me if I interviewed him. They were right, but I had to admire this man who almost every day visits the sick and the confined, just to offer them comfort. When I called on him, he was painting the interior of his cozy Dutch colonial house where he lives alone, his dining table covered with Bibles, religious tracts, and pamphlets.

Stiles Tobias, retired vice-president of Woolrich Woolen Mills, slowly and deliberately unfolded interesting scenes from his life and the life of the company. Of course, Woolrich is a revered institution in central Pennsylvania, so one has nothing bad to say about it. Like many older informants, Tobias seemed to recall events of sixty years ago more vividly than more recent events, even events of twenty or forty years ago. Or was it just his youth he recalled? He was very stimulated by the interview and immediately went out and read my earlier book, *Flatlanders and Ridgerunners.* Later, several people told me that Tobias has told the same stories at various board meetings over the years.

Some storytellers came to me. Dr. William Todhunter, a surgeon, called me after reading *Flatlanders,* and before he knew it, I was on his porch with my tape recorder running. He meant to talk mostly about his camp days up on Pine Creek but the words and images just didn't come. Instead, memories of his childhood in the Johnston area coal fields came flooding back and took shape in the light of his own words.

George Baker introduced himself after a talk I had given at the Williamsport Kiwanis Club. Months later, I visited his home to find out what was on his mind. Thirty years of writing federal farm loans had given him an insight into the dairy business. Baker knew the economic history of nearly every farm in Clinton, Lycoming, Tioga, and Sullivan counties.

My favorite storyteller in *Flatlanders* is Shorty Goodwin of Holliday, jack-of-all-trades and master yarn spinner. But the day we got together, he was preoccupied; he had his aged mother on his mind, visitors were coming, and a neighbor wanted him to trap coyotes. No stories sprouted that day; he talked mostly about his life.

Lisa Bainey of Emporium once gave me a list of

people to interview in Cameron and Elk counties. Slowly I have worked through the list, finding them all first-rate informants. The list includes Norm Erickson, Robert Lyon, Doc Dornish, and Dick Sassaman, a forest technician working out of Emporium.

My visit to Sassaman's isolated home was memorable. The woods loom so dark between Lock Haven and Emporium that the tiny towns seem like pricks of light in the darkness. Deer stand in the road, mile after mile, as if to say: "What are you doing here?" Sassaman's basement is a combination of trophy room, study, and gameroom. Turtle shells, turkey legs, frogs, and mounted pike, trout, bass, and muskie heads hang from the rafters. Bearskins, elk antlers, rattlesnake skins, bird feathers, and animal jawbones cover the walls. Sassaman talked in his deep voice for four hours. His love of wildlife and the wilderness captures what this country can mean to the people who live in north-central Pennsylvania.

Shot for a Woodchuck
Harry Clark, Collomsville

Now, I got absolute proof that my family the Clarks came over on the Mayflower. Why, they've been in this country for ever so long. They settled here in the Nippenose Valley when the Indian raids were still going on. Some people in my family were massacred by Indians in a raid during the French and Indian War in the 1750s.

My father made a lot of money in the lumber business, and during the boom era he got rich. That's when he bought the farm down the road by the mill and planned to put down roots. He was sixty-two years old, with more spunk in him than the hubs of hell. Now, the owner of the farm wanted to sell Dad the farm on the condition that Dad marry his daughter, Rose. She was about forty and had a face that would stop a clock. I mean her chances of swimming upstream to spawn were as good as a snowball's chances in hell. Well, Dad let on like, sure, he would marry her. He even started courting her, so then the farmer sold him the farm. As soon as he bought the farm, though, he announced that he was going to marry an eighteen-year-old girl from Williamsport.

My father and that young girl had seven kids together, and I am one of them. That woman was my mother. She's dead now; they both are.

What about Rose? Strangely enough, not long after Dad jilted her, she was courted by a nice man from over in Antes Fort. They were seen together for about six months and then they got married. It was sad though, real sad. All that marital bliss, that long-awaited sweetness was short-lived for Rose. One day her husband was high up in the mowing field with just the brown top of his hair showing, and some idiot down below, intent on shooting every woodchuck, mistook his hair for the hairy hide of a chuck and blew his head clean off. Yes sir, Rose's groom was shot for a woodchuck and that ended that romance.

The Calico Dress
John Youngmans, Williamsport

The Youngmans and the Antes families came together over a calico dress. It happened like this. The Antes family came to the Jersey Shore area long before the Revolutionary War. In the early 1800s, John Henry, Jr., and his wife had a daughter, Amelia, and they also adopted a daughter. Now, Amelia was clever with a needle, so her parents sent her to a lady in Newberry to learn to be a seamstress. The cost of her training was a heifer, so they put her on a raft and she floated downstream to Williamsport with the cow. She was about sixteen years old at the time, and the lady she was going to study with was named Reynolds.

A few weeks later, Amelia came back wearing a very fine calico dress she had made. She looked so pretty the adopted daughter was upset. They took to arguing with each other; there was no peace in the house. Finally, to restore calm, John Henry sent Amelia to visit her relatives in a place known as Jungman's Stettel. Today it is Mifflinburg.

Alone, Amelia rode her horse over the mountains. She must have made quite an impression in her calico dress, because in a few months she became engaged to Elias Pontius Youngman. (Youngman is

205

the American way of saying Jungman.) They married and moved back to Antes Fort, near the Jersey Shore–Williamsport area where their descendants have flourished.

Runaway Recruit
John Youngmans, Williamsport

It was just before the Battle of Gettysburg in the summer of 1863. The Union Army made a big push to enlist new men, and they got recruits from logging camps and the northern settlements. One day a long train full of these new enlisted men, thousands of them, pulled into downtown Williamsport. Back then, the tracks used to run right along Market Street downtown, and on that day all these men were hanging out of these cattle cars— and of course they were all drunk. Well, the children came from all over town to see the raw recruits. My relative was there with his son, and little Billy begged his father to hold him up to the train so he could see the men. "Where are you going?" he said to the men.

"We are off to fight the rebels," said the men.

"Take me with you! I want to go with you! Take me, Take me!" Billy yelled.

A group of soldiers took the boy from his father's arms and lifted him into the car. But Charlie, the boy's father, ran along (because the train was pulling out now) and tried to hold on to the boy's feet. But

Billy pushed his father away with his feet and squirmed up onto the train.

And that was the last they saw or heard of him until long after the war was done. For nearly four years they thought he was dead. Then one day he appeared in his uniform, a handsome young man. He told them his adventures and how he had been the servant of a captain.

The Flood on Antes Creek
John Youngmans, Williamsport

Three miles south of Jersey Shore, along the road that leads to Sugar Valley, Antes Creek slices through Bald Eagle Ridge at a place known as the Gap. Antes Creek, the only limestone stream in Lycoming County, comes bubbling up out of the ground at a place we call Enchanted Spring on Clyde Carpenter's place. It takes all the water from the Nippenose Valley—twelve or thirteen streams—and they sink down to an underground lake and then all come up in this one place. Then they flow down to the West Branch of the Susquehanna right where Antes Fort used to be during the Revolutionary War.

In the Gap stand two cut-limestone buildings, both dating back to the beginning of the nineteenth century. East of the road is a well kept inn, once the secret storehouse of Prince Farrington's Prohibition whiskey. Today it serves as an antique shop. West of the road, beside Antes Creek, the ruins of a large mill rise up among the sumach. For nearly a century

207

the mill ground flour for the farms in the nearby valleys.

It was May 31, 1867, and the family was staying in the cabin along Antes Creek because they had all been to a big celebration in Jersey Shore. George and Will were worried about the milldam a half mile upstream. The cabin lay on a flat below the millpond. If the dam should let go, they could get caught in the flood. Now, every stream and pond was full from heavy rains over the last few days.

The men put their children to bed and walked upstream to check out the dam. The water in the millpond was surging against the dam, but it looked strong enough to hold. So they went back to sleep. But while they slept something terrible happened. At about 2:00 A.M. that night, a huge downpour made the water rise even more. Water began to rush over the dam tearing up trees and twisting them across the creek below the dam. When the milldam broke, the water rushed out and ran into that pile of trees across the creek. The water rushed sideways over the bank and right at the cabin. Inside it must have been horrible. Little boys and girls were trying to get out, trying to swim, drowning. Out of the eleven people in the cabin that night, only four survived. Uncle Bill and Uncle George and two boys who were good swimmers got out alive.

Seven children drowned. I remember when first I learned of this. I was with my mother in the family cemetery, and I saw all these graves for our family dated May 31, 1867. When I asked her what happened, she told what I have just told you.

That is why I had such an interest in the dikes

along the river in Williamsport. Flood protection is a personal thing with me.

Peddlers in the Lumber Camps
Phil Marks, Renovo

A round Towanda, folks used to sing a ballad about Jake Marks who was ambushed and murdered on a lonely mountain road back in the early years of the century. Jake was my uncle, and he owned a clothing store in Towanda. Two Lebanese immigrants killed him for his money while he was on his way home to celebrate Passover. Jake's body was found many days later, but some people had an idea who had done it. My uncle Lou, Jake's brother, hired two Pinkerton detectives to follow the trail of the murders. Accompanying the detectives into Canada, Lou identified the killers coming out of a hotel in Toronto. The murderers were brought back to Laporte, and they were tried, convicted and hanged in the town square.

My father fled from Lithuania in 1892 because the tzar was repressing the Jews. He followed other family members to central Pennsylvania and immediately began peddling clothes to the logging camps and small rural communities. Back then, the trains reached almost everywhere; he would ride the trains with his goods, then he would backpack them into the camps. While he spoke English with a heavy Yiddish accent, he also spoke five other languages—a real advantage with all the immigrants

209

from Europe. In the mining and lumber camps, he sold woolen mittens, socks, heavy jackets, hats, and pants.

After years of riding the trains and hiking the back roads, he finally bought a horse and wagon for his goods. He kept using this wagon long after the automobiles took over. My father, Sol Marks, was well suited for the life of a peddler: he was strong and independent, he didn't like being pinned down, and he liked to keep his transactions to himself. Like many small American businessmen back then, he was self-reliant and liked it that way. Of course, peddling could be lonely and dangerous. Sol's friend, the peddler Harry Weinstein, was killed by a train at Cook's Run in the 1920s. In general, though, my father seemed to thrive on being outside in wind and weather and in making friends with the hard-working immigrant families back up in the mountains.

My father never seemed prosperous while he was peddling, but in fact he was making a lot of money. When the IRS would audit him, they would always send him back for more records. By 1916 he was invited to sit on the board of directors of the local bank, so he must have had money. He opened an account with Woolrich Woolen Mills on February 12, 1903, and that account—still active—is the oldest Woolrich account in Clinton County. My family has personally known four generations of the Rich family.

One day my father called Woolrich to place an order, and he heard the voice of a young boy on the line. "How old are you, boy?" he asked.

"I'm thirteen years old, sir," the boy said.

"What! You should be working in the mill, not on the phone," my father said. "What's your name, boy?"

"Sir, my name is Woods Rich," the boy said.

Woods Rich went on to become the president of Woolrich and a good friend of my father and me. So my father got to know some of the powerful people in the area, and he also got to know the men in the camps up in the hollows. Now, the towns were much bigger and busier around the turn of the century and even after the war. Take the town of Bitumen six miles up the road: today few houses remain; sixty years ago thousands lived there, working and shopping and drinking and getting married. In fact, one night in a saloon two men got to fighting and one stabbed the other and killed him. My father heard about it next day on the train back from Williamsport, where he often went on business. Talking with the county sheriff and district attorney about the crime on the ride home, my father asked the names of the men. When told, he said, "Why, I know those men. They were good fellows. I can't believe one would hurt the other."

The thing came to trial a few weeks later, and Sol got a subpoena to appear in court as a character witness for the accused. Dad didn't want to go because he was real shy about public appearances, but his testimony helped get the man's sentence reduced. At least he didn't hang.

I am seventy-one years old now. My family has had a clothing store in Renovo since before I was born. Now, this town has treated us well, and we gave something back to the town, I believe. The big problem with the town came with the strike of 1922. I remember that day because I was five years old and had just been vaccinated for the first time. I can see the men walking out of the shops now, heading home. They thought it would soon be over, but the union lost out. It was a lot like the paper company strike in Lock Haven going on right now. It was never the same after the strike. Lots of men went back to work on the sly. The town was divided, and of course, the timber was finished then, and the railroad in decline. It really was the end of an era. But as long as the engine shops were running full bore, people believed nothing bad could happen to the town. In that sense, Renovo was a one-industry town.

A Hill Farmer's Life
Veris Metzger, Salladasburg

We had a good life up here on the top of the mountain. After my parents died, the three boys farmed and we never married. We raised potatoes, wheat, oats, buckwheat, corn, and rye. We made butter and peddled it along with milk and eggs in Jersey Shore. As long as we didn't plow the fields too wide, the soil was all right.

If we plowed too much and didn't leave swaths of grass in between them, the field would start to erode. Because we're on the mountaintop, the water runs off fast. If a cut, as we called it, got started in the field, we had a heck of a time stopping it. We had to fill it in with brush and stone—otherwise, the cut would eat away the whole field. Many's the time we had to put boulders and brush in a spot where the rain started running and cutting into the soil.

I loved growing up on a farm. I loved the work of it. I loved watching things grow. I went to common school for a few years but I hated it. We got our first tractor, an Allis Chalmers, in 1941. Up to then, we farmed by hand. One of us could plow an acre and a half a day with a horse and plow. You'd tie the reigns over your shoulder or behind your back and hold on to the plow. You had to be careful that the horses didn't break on you. They could yank you over the plow and you could get buggered up on the plow as you fell over. "Plow deep while sluggards sleep, and you'll have corn to sell and keep." We used to say that. We'd plant potatoes by the dark of the moon so the bugs wouldn't eat them. I believe that. Now, why do we want to go messing with the moon for? If God wanted a man on the moon he would have built a road there. I get a hundred thirty-five dollars a month from the Social Secure, and I sure can't afford to live there.

Any signs are important to planting. "Red sky at night, sailor's delight; red sky at morning, sailor take warning." The end of the month you could read like this. "Mary went over the mountain wet; she came back dry." If the month ended wet, look for six months of dry weather. If dry, then look for rain.

Horses were real important to us. They were the spokes that made the wheel turn on a farm. Here's a story: These poor folks had a old horse they rode into town with a load of pumpkins—their only cash

213

crop. They sold the pumpkins, but instead of buying food for the horse, they bought whiskey and got drunk. On the way home they challenged another wagon to a race. They whipped their horse as he ran until finally he gave out and died.

And here's another true story about horses. My grandpa knew a good horse when he saw one, so one day he went into Williamsport to get the better of a horse trader. Now, that was mighty hard to do—beat them at their own game. Horse traders then were like used car dealers today. They could bring a horse in on a stretcher, feed it some arsenic to perk it up, shine it all up, and get it ready to show. A few hours after it was sold, it would roll over dead.

But Grandad knew all their tricks, and he knew horses by their feet, their teeth, their eyes, and their shape. So he traded some whiskey for a really good horse.

After we got the horse back to the farm, Grandpa called us all together and said, "Those horse traders will come and try to steal that horse back tonight. We'd best hide him in the blacksmith shop."

So for two weeks we hid the horse in various unlikely places around the farm. One morning we found the barn door had been left open and matches were on the floor where the thieves had come to look for the horse.

And speaking of whiskey, Prince Farrington supplied most of the whiskey back then. He had a still just over in the next hollow. One time, the moonshiner who worked for Prince got brought into court. They brought barrels of whiskey into the jail house, but when it came time for them to produce the evidence it was all gone. People said the whiskey was so good that it all "leaked out."

In court, the judge said, "Mister, who do you sell your stuff to?"

"Why, your honor, I sell it to the mayor, Mr. Johnson, the baker, Mr. Smith, the preacher, Reverend Jones, and to you, Your Honor," the moonshiner said.

The judge let him go.

Mountain Fiddler
Harvey Wright, Lockwood

I'm so glad you come to see me. I don't play much any more, unless there's folks to get me in the spirit. My back is so bad now. I got this special chair I made to sit on. I go down to the chiropractor in town and he lays me down and gives me a sharp knee in the hip, like this, and my insides go right back in place and I start to feel all right for a while. Then I get in the truck, and by the time I'm back home it's hurting the same all over again.

Come on inside the trailer. Sure, it's messy, but it ain't really dirty. See, up here in the hills we keep some things right inside the livingroom, like chainsaws and gasoline and tools and lawnmowers. You never know what might go on outside here. The stuff could get stolen. But more likely it could get skunk pee or possum dribble on it. Hell, I've had porcupines eat my broom handles and woodchucks eat rubber hoses on my mower. You can't never tell up here.

We've always lived on this mountain. My father, grandfather, our family has been here for over a hundred and seventy years. They marched up with General Sullivan in the 1780s when he came up to wipe out the Iroquois for the Wyoming Valley Massacre. Yep. They saw the land and they liked it. It was given to the soldiers after the war as a sort of payment. My grandparents came from England in the early 1800s. That was on my mother's side. Both sides were English. I was born in 1908. They had been on this mountain for a long time then.

Everyone in the family lived on the mountain on the hillside. That is just the way we lived. It was private, and it saved the good land for the farm. The ground didn't stay wet for a long time, either. They had ten kids, my mother and father.

I remember when Dad bought five fiddles from a Jewish Peddler. They all needed fixing. Paid five dollars for them. You couldn't get the one he gave me out of my hands. He fixed a nice one up and gave it to me. Both he and my grandfather were great fiddlers, and I wanted to become a great fiddler too. They got me off to a good start. Did my poor mother suffer! The hardest thing was getting in tune. You had to use the pegheads then. You had to use some muscle pushing and twisting the pegs on the old fiddles. They didn't have the little adjusters they have now.

One day I tried so hard to tune my fiddle that I broke the peghead right off. My father was a good carver and he fixed it all up right and glued it back on. After that, you had to break it someplace else because you couldn't break it there.

I was nine when I started playing. I've played music all my life. Could have learned to read music and make some money, but I just never got around to it. I played better without reading music. What I heard I could play. Now, I always gave my music away. I never charged anybody for hearing me, and if I played a dance, they could pay me or not—I didn't care. It was a joy in me that made me play. There was music in the fiddle that wanted to get out and I just helped it along. I just played what was in my head.

You didn't hear that much music back then, so when you did hear it live, you tended to remember it. Oh, Lord, I know more tunes than I forgot. Somebody play it and I'll play it too. I don't go by the name, just the sound of it.

When my father was a very old man, he got kind of crazy. They couldn't control him, so they came and took him off the mountain and took him to the county home where they put the loonies. It was the dead of winter then. I was in my late fifties when this happened. He still had the strength of his youth on him when he was in his seventies. They say it was from playing the fiddle all those years. Anyway, he bent back the bars on the windows, jumped out of a second story window, and disappeared into a blizzard, figuring that they couldn't track him in the snow. He showed up the next morning in his house on the mountain. He got down his gun and his fiddle and put them on the kitchen table. He played his fiddle while he waited for them to come and get him, but they never did. He got better after that and died a natural death two years later.

Anyway, let's play some of my favorite tunes: how about "Fisher's Hornpipe," "Rochester Schottische," "Durang's," "Turkey in the Straw," "Fever in the Creek," "Fireman's Dance," "Over the Waves"—hell, there's a bunch of them. Did you notice that I don't even have a pinky on my left hand? Neat trick to note with no pinky, my friend. I chopped it off one February night when I was cutting kindling after drinking some moonshine. Hurt like hell for about three weeks, but it didn't hurt my fiddling none, not in the long run.

The Fiddle with Music in It
Harry D'Addario, New Berlin

From my earliest days I loved the violin. When we would go to the country dances as children, I would always go up to the fiddler when he quit playing and ask to touch the strings. "Go ahead," the German man would say. "You can touch the strings."

"Do you think he'll ever play?" my mother asked him once.

"This one? Of course he'll play, and he'll play good," he said.

Somehow my oldest brother got hold of a fiddle, but he just couldn't figure out how to play it. I think he knew I would be able to play it, so he didn't want me to touch it. Then I got a boil on my shin and I had to stay home from school for a week. What a week! I played all day, and I started getting the music out of that fiddle. When my brother found out, what a row we had. But after that I never stopped playing, and soon I had my own fiddle.

Middleburg had a lot of Germans, and Dad Rau and Calvin Walters taught me how to play like this—slow with only a shuffle here and there. We played schottisches and waltzes and everything.

If they wanted to have a square dance, they'd come and get me. Money? Ha! They didn't have any money back then. You'd play for free, or they would give you a treat or something. We'd play "Arkansas Traveler," "St. Anne's Reel," "Soldier's Joy," "Liberty," "Ragtime Annie," "Turkey in the Straw," and others. The callers did the singing calls and we all liked that, but the musicians had to "rhyme" the tune to the caller so the dancers would come around on time.

One fiddle and two guitars, or two fiddles and one guitar usually made up the dance band. Later we added a potato bug—a mandolin with a round back. I played that one myself. I didn't see a banjo until the 1920s and that was a four-string—the kind we still use in the Union County String Band today.

There's a story behind every fiddle I ever owned. Now, the first time I played a really good fiddle was in Freyburg. Mr. Meyer, the music store owner there, called me over and asked me to play four new fiddles he just got in from Italy. They were made by Carlos Scarelli in Milan. "Go ahead and play all of them, go ahead," he said.

The best fiddle I ever got was given to me by Reno Beaver's wife after he died. "Take it," she said, "and play it, only promise me you will never sell it."

So I played it and I played it. That fiddle had so much music in it. Reno was a World War I soldier and he paid eighty-five dollars for that fiddle at Rever's Music Store in Sunbury before the war. Do you want to play it? I can still hear Reno play "The Kingdom" on that fiddle when I look at it.

Then there was Napoleon Brosius, another fiddler who I used to see when I was working as a dairy inspector. "To hell with work, Harry, sit down and play a couple of tunes with me," he always used to say.

People always wanted me to sit down and play with them, and it's still like that today. The Rosedale Dairy where I had worked for many years went out of business when I was about sixty-three, so I got a job as custodian at Bucknell University in Lewisburg. Boy, I made a lot of friends there. I just retired, but I often go back and visit.

While I was at Bucknell, something happened that got the provost and even the president involved: after I finished my work as custodian, the foreman didn't mind what I did with the time remaining on my shift. I usually had an hour or two of free time, so I would play my fiddle.

Soon the word went out that I could fiddle pretty good. Some students and a few professors would come over and jam with me. Professor Bob Taylor, the one who writes novels, would play the fiddle right along with me. One night we had over fifty people there jamming and dancing in the halls. Some of the profs and the foreman thought that was too much fun. Better put a stop to it, they said. So we quit. But when Wendell Smith, the provost, and

Charlie Watts, the president, heard about it, they put their heads together and said, "If he's finished his work and he isn't bothering anybody, then let him play. He's teaching the students and profs how to play, and God knows we could use some more fiddlers around here."

So we went back to playing.

The Sawmill at Nesbit Farm
Charlie Simpson, Nesbit

Yes, I grew up in the last days of the great log boom. I recall riding on a wagon with my father into Williamsport along the River Road and you could see nothing but logs for miles in the river. Men who worked on the river were called boom rats. My Dad was one for a while. I used to hear them joking, "Always wear two layers of wool clothes 'cause if you fall in, the wool will still keep you warm," they'd say. It wasn't great work, but what else was there?

Later on, my father opened a small sawmill right here. First it ran on water and then on steam.

Back then we had a powwow—a healer over in Loganton—and he could cure just about anything. Stomachache, the grippe, warts—he could cure them all. One time I had a hernia, and I went on over and he put his hand on it and gave me some herb and said some words and burned some incense. Pretty soon it went away. Yes, and we had midwives

221

too: Mrs. Usler and Mrs. Ulrich and then later a doctor. We was all born right here in this house.

Back then, we worked for each other in Nesbit; all through this century, everybody knew everybody else and nobody went hungry. Why, if you were sick they'd be folks doin' your chores for you. It worked good that way. Of course, we had only a couple hundred of us in Nesbit then. Now there's about a thousand folks here. It's got mighty crowded.

During the Depression, nobody went hungry. We were small dairy farmers back then, and we raised cash crops of wheat and grain. We didn't need much. We traded the wheat at the gristmill in town for flour. We traded for a keg of nails, spices, coffee, tea, and dress material. They had a nail mill in South Williamsport then, and we had a general store here where you could buy just about anything. Cohick's Store up in Salladasburg is close to what the old general stores were like.

We raised most of our food right here on the farm, so the Depression didn't hit us really. We gave many and many a bushel of food away. Nobody starved around here. You see, that's the good thing about living on a farm: you always have something to eat. The bad thing is that you always have something to do. I've never stopped working all my life. Never had much time for anything.

In the winter we would butcher the hogs and beef. Half the meat we ate was pork. Game was scarce then. Must have been the logging drove it away. Now it's back. Well, we'd kill a hog on a cold day and freeze some of it for eating in the winter, but the pork we wanted to save for a long time we would cure in this way: we would make a brine and soak the hams in the brine. Now, we knew when the brine was thick enough with salt when an egg would float with just a round spot the size of a dime showing above the water. Then she was OK. We'd let that homecure four or five weeks until the salt drawed out all the blood. Then we'd hang it up and smoke it real slow over a blend of hickory and sassafras fire for three days. Oh, yes, you could use oak or maple, but sassafrass was the best. I can taste it now. We'd have it cold on a summer evening— you couldn't beat it.

Now my dad died when he was sixty-seven of a heart attack while sleeping in his bed. "I want to die in the harness," he said.

Nobody in my family smoked, but Dad chewed, and yet we never saw him spit—and he didn't swallow it, neither. He was a sawyer but he had all his fingers. They say a sawyer will always have fingers missing. They get nipped by the blades. Hell, every piece of machinery around a farm is dangerous. That corn shucker right there is a dangerous devil. Friend of mine lost his hand a few years back. They were picking one cold frosty morning. Hired hand said, "I ain't goin to pull the husks out of that thing. I might slip." The husks was jamming the shucker. So the farmer went over and tried it, and didn't it pull him in and mash his hand? They had to cut it off. He has a hook now but he's still working.

When I was a boy we did everything by hand. We didn't get a tractor here until 1938. There it is. A John Deere and it still runs perfect, as long as you keep good oil in it.

Before then, we did it all by hand. Cut wood? That's half my life. We never stopped cutting wood, and in winter we'd cut ice down there in the river.

I plowed many an acre by hand with this bull-tongue plow. It wasn't so bad when the field was good, but when it was rocky it was tough—holding them horses back and keeping the furrow straight—it was tough. We always raised wheat, and we'd harvest the grain with a mowing scythe. This one here with the little arms sticking out of the handle of the scythe above the blade—we called that the cradle. Well, you was talking about them old fiddle tunes, and that one called "Rock the Cradle, Joe." That's not about a baby cradle, that's about cutting wheat. They called it "rocking the cradle" when we were cutting the wheat by hand with a scythe. Yessir, I could rock the cradle all day long.

The best thing about living here all these years is where it is. You look below you, and there's the blue river rolling by. You look behind you, and there's Bald Eagle Mountain and the green fields in between. I wouldn't swap it, no sir.

A Pine Creeker Is a Pine Creeker
Billy Wolfe, Slate Run

I was born in 1914 and went to this one-room schoolhouse on the cliff overlooking Pine Creek at Slate Run. Since my father was away, we kids had to shift for ourselves. We were doing odd jobs from day one. I recall stealing coal from the trains when the

men would stop to have lunch. We'd climb up the
ladder and toss coal down. That's how we heated our
house. I hopped freights, too, as a boy. Even though
freight hopping was illegal, the conductor said to me
once, "Billy, when you hop on or off, grab hold of
the bar and get your feet running with the train first,
then hop on or off. Otherwise, you will skin your
knee."

Growing up in Slate Run was just fine. We had a
few hundred people here and the same at Camel
and Cedar Run. We sledded and skated in winter,
fished and swam in summer, hunted and hiked in
fall. Chores were like games to us back then. I
remember the big Tome picnic—a reunion of all
the Tome relatives. Phillip Tome, the famous elk
and panther hunter, settled along Pine Creek in
the 1790s. Hundreds of his descendants used to
come to the reunion every year. The Hillburns and
the Gambles and the Wolfes were all related. Each
group brought its own food, and they built a
pavilion for the musicians. Fiddles and banjos and
dancing, then baseball and sack races with a
couple of drunks rolling around in the dirt. Then
all the old-timers began to die out and after the
Second World War they stopped having the
reunion. Then they tried Old Home Day, but that
fizzled out.

Now, once they played a trick on Mr. Pauke, an
Italian fellow who made wine during Prohibition.
One day he walked into the railroad station and
overheard the stationmaster say over the phone,
"Help, send a doctor right away. Buck Kniveson has
drunk some of Pauke's bad wine and he's dying."

Pauke took it seriously and ran right across Pine Creek screaming at his wife, "Get rid of the stuff. Kniveson is dead and they're coming to get me."

The Cake Walk and the Box Lunch Social were used to raise money for schoolbooks. The ladies would all bring boxes of food and the hunters from out of town would come and bid on the boxes. They sat with the woman who made the dinner they bought, only they couldn't tell who made what. So they would ask us boys, and we would get them all mixed up so they ended up sitting with the old ladies and not the pretty young girls.

Working on the highway, I had eighty-four miles of road to keep clear, and some winters it was rough. Along the high cliff above Cedar Run where the guard rails are washed out, we had to back the cinder truck uphill after a snowstorm. Once while shoveling cinders out the back, I slipped, fell out of the truck, and started sliding down the cliff into Pine Creek. It's three hundred feet down. Finally, they found me and rescued me from a tiny ledge.

After living up here in Slate Run for over seventy years, I still get a kick out of the outsiders who move up here and try to civilize us. They want to improve on police protection, fire protection, public transportation, garbage disposal—the works. It's as though we've been living in darkness all these years. Often we let them have their way so they can learn city thinking just doesn't work up here. Up here, things get done by neighbors talking to neighbors. We work things out. Pine Creekers know how to live, but the outsiders take forever to learn our ways—if they can.

226

Freight-Hopping Along
the Susquehanna
Lester Pfirman, Nesbit

Trains were the big thing along the West Branch when I was a boy in Nesbit. Trains rolled through town night and day, but the logging was mostly over along the river. Before World War I, they were dredging the sand out of the river with steam barges and shipping it out on the trains. From Avis you could take a train to Lock Haven, Williamsport, Harrisburg, just anywhere.

About two hundred people lived in Avis back then. Some farmed and others worked on the railroad. When I was a kid, I worked cleaning out coal cars. It was dusty work, and so I started chewing Tiger Tobacco. I was afraid my father would catch me. Then one day he saw me and said, "Give me a cut of that stuff, boy." He figured the work was dusty and a chew was OK.

In 1918 the influenza epidemic came. We had a local powwow, but he couldn't stop it. Boy I worked with died. I got it and just barely made it. Been living ever since.

We had a blacksmith named Bussler in Nesbit then. He could shoe any horse and never drive a nail into the nerve in the hoof. Horse goes nuts when you hit the nerve. Like a tooth. Bussler could make any tool. He never swore. "By the life," or "By the Eternal" were the only oaths he would say. One time I saw a horse kick him clear out of his shop and out into a puddle in the street. When he made a wagon

227

wheel tire out of iron, he'd slip it on the wooden
wheel while it was red hot and drop it into a water
pan. The hot iron would shrink while it cooled and
fit tight as a drum around the wooden rim.

In July and August we used to catch trout along
Benders Run where the mill wheel was. Had to be
careful, though, 'cause copperheads and rattlesnakes
came down off Bald Eagle Mountain if it was dry. I
darn near stepped on a couple. The waterwheel was
still at the gristmill in the summer, but when a
bunch of us went for a swim we liked to get the big
waterwheel turning. The paddle that had been in the
water was always waterlogged, so we'd work the
wheel around by hand until the heavy section got to
the top and then let her go. Well, one time we let
her go, and somehow I was in the water and too
close to the wheel when it came down and I got
pinned between the wheel and the side. My head
was stuck under water and almost crushed. I was
under for a long time, and I was starting to lose
consciousness. Then somehow the wheel turned back
and I slipped out with my head all bloody. I still
have the lump from it here.

I went into the woods with my uncle to skid logs
sometimes. He had two big horses he used for
skidding, and—boy—did they know what they were
doing. When they were pulling a log down a steep
skid and it started running down on them from
behind, they knew enough to jump to the side and
get out of the way. Then, as the log skidded by,
they'd brace themselves and the grabs holding the
chain would pop out of the log and the log would go
crashing on by. This worked for them for years until

one day a huge log slid down and they couldn't pop the grabs. It pulled the horses down the hill and mangled both of them.

Hopping freights was my specialty when I was a kid. Now, you had to be careful. You could get killed real easy. One time, I was coming back from Williamsport with my friend Lawrence Hewitt. He was new to freight hopping. We got on all right because the train had stopped. In fact, we had to climb up on the catwalk on top of the car to hide from the railroad police.

I can remember lying there, getting rust all over my new suit. And that was only the beginning. Now, when the train started to roll, the next thing on my mind was getting off. If the train was slowing down or stopping at Nesbit, it was no problem. But if it was going on through to Lock Haven or Renovo, then we had problems. I could tell by Duboistown that this was a fast freight—probably with those new Santa Fe engines—and it wasn't going to stop. We would have to make a hard landing.

Now, getting off or getting on a moving train, the big thing to remember was to go for the front part of the car. That way, if you missed, the car would "bounce" you off the track. If you grabbed for the end of a car and missed, the car behind would smack you. I explained all this to Lawrence and I put him at the front of the car and I took the rear. "When you hit just try to run; if you can't run fast enough, then roll," I told him.

By the time we approached Nesbit, it was just about dark and she was moving fast. We had to jump or end up God knows where. I waved to Lawrence to jump and I saw him hit, bounce, and roll over and over. I thought sure he was dead. Then I let go, and when I hit I thought I was a goner, too. Seems I rolled forever. I came to in the middle of the eastbound track with cinder burns all over my hands. I lay there. Then I moved. I could move everything. When I found Lawrence, he was all right. We limped home just glad to be alive, but when I came in, my mother saw blood all over my leg and screamed. I'd been cut in the leg but the suit wasn't scratched—just bloody. That was my last bit of freight hopping.

Track Walker for the Railroad
Louie Stanley, Nesbit

I was born in a log house along Benders Run here in Nesbit, and I ain't lived anyplace else. Back in the old days, in the 1920s, we had a millrace in the run here and a water wheel that we used to grind corn and we could use it to saw, too. We'd let a rush of water through so the wheel would turn and the machinery would go. Then we'd have to wait until the water built up again. I worked for thirteen cents a day.

The railroad came through in 1924 and that changed things. I went to work as a lineman on the railroad. I remember the great flood of 1936 and I remember clearing twelve-foot drifts of snow off the tracks. I started out aligning track. A crew of us

230

would walk along and straighten out the rails and ties with long iron bars. We'd pry them back in place. Lowly work it was for a railroad man. Later on, I became a track walker and I'd walk the line looking for trouble spots.

The railroad life was steady work, but it could be dangerous. One track walker was killed by a train one night right along here. We never quite knew how. He didn't hear the train somehow. Sound does strange things along the railroad. Jerry Cox was killed while he was cleaning and oiling a switch one day in a snowstorm right down here below Nesbit. Now, we had three tracks going along the river: one went east, one west, and one was a siding. The rule of the company was this: when you're working in the rails and you hear a train coming along, you have to get clear of *all* the tracks. It's a good rule and here's why. When trains are coming from opposite directions, you can only hear one. The one you're looking at is the only one you will think is bearing down on you. Now, that's what happened to Billy. He looked up from the switch and saw a slow freight rolling down the line. The wind was howling and snow was falling. When the train he was watching got near. He just stepped over onto the other track without looking back and an express train caught him blind.

George Shetler called to me, "Louie, Billy's been run over; let's go down and see if we can help."

I said no. I knew I just couldn't bear to look at him.

Once I was ordered to drive the crew truck down the tracks to pick up a work crew at Antes Fort.

This truck was a regular truck, but you could drive it along the tracks. I double-checked with the dispatcher and he told me no trains were coming. So I got my permit and drove the crew truck down towards Antes Fort. Well, I picked up twenty men working on the tracks, turned around, and headed on back. We were getting near South Williamsport when what should I see but a passenger train rounding the bend heading right at us. I yelled, "Train coming!"

We all jumped off the truck. We were so scared we just heaved and lifted the truck off the tracks. A few seconds later, the train whistled on by. Oh, that dispatcher was a wreck after that. You see, he could have gone to jail if we'd been killed. I ripped the pants off the dispatchers after that one, I did.

Now, back in the old days you had two kinds of folks in Nesbit, the drinkers and card players, and the religious people. I married Anna Crossley, and she never set foot on a dance floor. Back then, we used to go free to the Billy Sunday meetings in Williamsport. Oh, it would lift up the soul! Nevertheless, in Nesbit we had a house of prostitution where the men would go, black and white. We had a hotel that sold liquor after Prohibition was repealed, and before that a big moonshiner who worked with Prince Farrington, the famous bootlegger from Jersey Shore.

Now, I have always spoken out against whiskey and cards, which are the devil's tools. I have seen people like my brother die of the shakes or delirium tremens and it's not a pretty sight. Bus Bussler was a blacksmith in town here, a hard-working man who could make any tool you wanted, and he had a nice wife and he played the fiddle. One day he turned to drink: he shot up his house with a shotgun, and then he went crawling down the road in the mud. Next day, he lay sweating and dying. They called me because I always prayed over the sick. "Louie, I'm afraid to die," Bus said.

I prayed with him and he died peacefully.

Yes, I still visit the sick and go to the homes in Williamsport about twice a week to pray with them. I see the real bad ones too, but it tuckers me out to see them.

A Life with Woolrich
Stiles Tobias, Woolrich

I was born in 1899 in Mackeyville, and we soon moved to Woolrich where my father worked. I grew up in a fine company house right across from the Woolrich Woolen Mill. Ellery Channing Tobias, my father, worked as a Woolrich salesman in the southern Appalachians, opening up new territories like West Virginia and Eastern Kentucky. He had it in his head that he wanted to be somebody and he didn't mind the hours. Working his way up over the years, my father became president of the company and chairman of the board of directors.

In summer I worked at the woolen mills from six in the morning to six at night. After grade school, four of us went on to high school in Lock Haven: we walked three miles from Woolrich to McElhattan to catch the morning train, went to school, and returned by the six o'clock train, then walked back to Woolrich at about seven at night. After high school I attended the Philadelphia Textile Institute, and when I graduated I went to work for Woolrich as a salesman in 1920. My father and Mr. Rich decided I should get experience by selling in the southern mountain states. At this time the logging industry had moved south, into the great forests of the southern Appalachians. The Woolrich Company still concentrated on manufacturing heavy outerwear, so wherever men were working outdoors, especially in the logging camps, we brought our goods to the nearby stores. The company assigned me to sell in Maryland, Virginia, West Virginia, Tennessee, and Kentucky. Can you imagine? Of course, it just about killed me, but I tried it for about three years.

I can recall a typical sales trip for me back then. I targeted two remote logging camps in Eastern Kentucky where we had never been. The frigid winter would sell our two-piece woolen underwear by itself, I knew, so I filled my suitcases. After riding the Baltimore and Ohio along treacherous, steep mountain ridges for a day, I arrived in Kentucky at a seedy, primitive, railhead town. Then I waited a day for the logging train to return, because one could only reach the camps every other day. That night I donned woolen underwear and slept on the countertop of the general store. Such was mountain hospitality.

Next day I hitched a ride on the narrow-gauge logging train. Now, this train wasn't meant for passengers. I hopped on the little steam engine and watched her crawl the twelve miles into camp. At

the camp store, I sold out all I brought with me.
Then I ate the loggers' greasy food, drank their
strong coffee in the mess hall, sang their jolly songs
around the stove, and went to sleep that night in the
bunkhouse with men all around me snoring like
lions. After waiting a day, I rode the Shay engine
out, only this time I had to ride atop a pile of logs
behind an engine spewing rank smoke. By the time
we arrived at the town I was black as a tarbaby. I
had to rent a bath and towel, pay for my suit to be
cleaned, and put on my last clean clothes. All in a
day's work when selling in the mountains. A few
days later, I hiked twelve miles into another camp.

My father had opened up West Virginia for the
company before World War I. Now I found myself
back in his territory seeking out remote stores atop
mountains and up lonesome hollows. I recall one
time getting stranded at the top of a mountain
during a terrific storm. The folks wanted me to spend
the night there, but I had to push on. Rather than
backtrack on a safe road, I decided to drive down a
narrow dirt road clinging to a steep cliff. As I drove
out into the storm, I noticed trees blown down
everywhere. Somehow I got the car down the
mountain—only to find my way blocked by a giant
fallen hemlock. Now, the stump rose high above the
roadside, so I tried easing the car under the trunk,
but to no avail. Then I tried taking air out of the
tires—the old hard kind—but that didn't work,
either. Finally, I met a woodsman with an axe and
persuaded him to cut pieces out of the bottom of the
trunk so I could slip the car underneath and be on
my way. Then I had to pump up those tires again.

At first, all my travels and the challenge of opening up new territory for Woolrich clothes kept me going, but after three years of constant travel, I suffered a collapse from physical exhaustion. I returned to Woolrich and simply recuperated. A year and a half later, I hit the road again with a smaller territory and a man helper. I managed to return to Woolrich every three weeks to see my family. Great things were going on in Woolrich now. My father embarked on a huge building program for the town; together with his builder, Sheridan Cryder, my father designed and built over seventy homes for Woolrich, homes owned by the company and rented to its employees. Back then when the company employed only two hundred people, we all knew each other. Things were on a personal basis. Today, of course, with twenty-two hundred employees that family atmosphere isn't always possible.

After working as a salesman for over twenty years, in 1943 I began working at Woolrich as a wool buyer. The wool salesmen came right to the plant. Soon I learned all the different grades of wool from all over the world. We needed coarse wool for outer wear and very fine wool for expensive sweaters and certain wool for blankets. Each variety of sheep produced a different grade of wool. This job was my favorite.

Just after the war, my father became president of Woolrich, the first person outside the Rich family to hold the post. Bob Rich was elected to the United States Congress at the time, and he felt my father could do the best job. "Let Ellery Tobias run the company, since he knows more about it than anyone else," said Bob Rich.

My father was seventy-five at the time, but he continued to run the company for many years, serving also as the chairman of the board of directors. Now, in 1973 I became a vice-president in the company, and in 1975 I was elected chairman of the board. This year I am eighty-nine years old. My life and the lives of many in my family have been intertwined with Woolrich. My son works as a third-generation salesman for Woolrich in Pennsylvania, and my grandson works in sales for Woolrich on the west coast. That's four generations working for Woolrich.

Now, from the time I started with Woolrich right up into the 1960s, the company continued to rely on heavy outerwear and winter wear as its bread and butter. But two men could see that focus was too narrow: the company needed to diversify, needed to make a variety of clothes for all seasons. Roswell Brayton and John Billington turned Woolrich from a single-minded company into the diverse producer of clothes and woolens it is today. They pushed Goretex jackets, slacks, nylon parkas, and sportswear. They began producing in the Orient, and they broadened our base here. Today we may produce too many different kinds of clothes, making stocking and reordering a big problem, but Brayton and Billington brought Woolrich up to date, kept us in stride with the modern world, and kept us growing. The company has grown every year since I joined it in 1920. The company stock has grown, too. That's a fine thing.

A Doctor's Story
William Todhunter, Williamsport

I was born in Barnsboro, in Cambria County, about thirty miles north of Johnston. I grew up in a family with twelve children. Out of two separate families a third family came into existence. But unlike the modern mixed family, it was death, not divorce that split up the first families. My mother gave birth to a son not long after her husband died in a mining cave-in. My father's first wife died in childbirth, leaving four girls and three boys. Somewhere the widow and widower met, courted, married, and had four more children, including me. We all grew up together and eleven out of twelve graduated from college.

The Todhunters came over from England when my father was eight. His mother died, so he followed his father from mine to mine in the Pennsylvania coal fields. Finally, my grandfather married a widow with four children, and another mixed family settled down happily, with all the boys working in the mines. Dad worked as a trap boy when he was twelve, opening and closing the mine doors for the mules pulling the coal cars. He made two-fifty a week and saved fifty cents for books. Although he only went to sixth grade, he read his way through mail-order courses on mining engineering and began to rise in the company. By the time I was a teenager, he was head operator of the Barnes and Tucker Mine. He later became president.

The mines were deep-pit or deep-shaft mines with

huge pumps pulling the water out. At the age of fourteen, me and all my brothers went to work outside the mine, and at sixteen we went inside. My father insisted we do mine work because he wanted us to know what hard work was and how men made a living. We worked summers and holidays until we went to college. Dad didn't want to take a job from the miners with families, so we had to work in the steel mills.

The life of a coal miner could be rough. A lot depended on the company: some treated their men poorly, forcing them to buy at the company store and deducting it from their pay. My father fought against that, persuading Barnes and Tucker to sell the company houses to the miners. What a blossoming came of that! They painted houses, planted trees and flowers, cut the grass, and built little fences. The miners were Hungarian, Polish, and Italian and spoke a broken English. They dug the soft coal with picks and blasted with dynamite, and later on they used cutting and loading machines. Miners earned ninety cents a ton and had to dig nine tons a day. As a young man, I can remember seeing Pete the Pumper, a real jolly fellow, one day just at dusk going down into the mine to check the pumps. Joking around with another miner as he walked into the shaft, he said, "I'll see you later and tell you the one about the mule and the parson."

We never saw him alive again. They had shut off the air pumps, but no one had blocked the entrance to the mine. Pete was asphyxiated by methane gas.

As teenagers, we played wild tricks with electricity, fireworks, and dynamite. Coal cars

needed sand to keep the tracks gritty, and the miners
would put their lunch boxes in the sand house to
keep them cool. We would run electric wires to the
lunch box of a new man and give him a jolt when
he hoisted out his box. We would slide firecrackers
down the pipes when men were carrying them,
and—Bam!—they would sound like a cannon. But
our favorite trick was waking up the baseball team
with dynamite. See, every big coal company had a
baseball team, like a semipro team. Competition
between companies was fierce, with lots of betting
and rivalries. Now, the ball players just hung around
during the season and played ball. During the day
they slept and lay around in a grove by the woods.
The miners resented this. At least once a summer we
would sneak up, dig a hole, fill it with dynamite,
cover it with small rocks, light the fuse, and run.
We loved to watch the men wake up and run before
the rocks started hitting the ground.

Another vivid memory from childhood comes from
Camp Cedar Pines up Pine Creek at Cedar Run. We
would play all day long at this wonderful place,
swimming in Pine Creek, hiking in the woods,
playing baseball and volleyball, working on crafts,
and going on overnight horseback rides in the Black
Forest.

My father insisted I attend Thiel College, but after
a year I persuaded him to let me switch to Allegheny
College where I could get a better premed education.
My girlfriend was there, too. We had been
sweethearts since the sixth grade, and we are still
married after all these years. After Allegheny, I
attended Temple Medical School. I remembered how

frightened we all were when the dean said a third of us would be gone by the year's end. The first year was extremely hard, but I wanted to be there. After medical school, I opened up a family practice in Williamsport. During the Great Depression, folks around here told me, "Williamsport has seventy industries—they can't all fail at once."

They were right. The town weathered the Depression amazingly well and began to boom again in the 1940s. By then, I was back at Temple for a three years' surgeon's residence. Finally, I returned to Williamsport where I set up a practice in surgery. Today I share my practice with my son.

Years ago, people would put up with ailments more than folks today. People endured sprains, coughs, even hernias. They weren't used to good doctoring and often got confused. Here's an example of what I mean. A man came to me with bowel trouble, so I X-rayed his colon. He needed a laxative, so I prescribed one, probably paregoric, telling him to take one a day before each evening meal. Then his wife chimed in and said he needed something for his nerves. He was a henpecked dog if ever I saw one. So I gave him a mild prescription for phenobarb, and said to take one four times a day. Well, two days later the lady is on the phone, and she says, "Oh doctor, my husband went down to the bank and shit his pants on the street, and he's shit all his pants now, and all our bed sheets are shitted. What should I do?—"

So I told her to bring him to the emergency room, and after talking to her I realized she had switched directions on the medicine. She was giving him four

241

doses of paregoric a day and her poor husband almost shitted himself to death.

The End of Small Dairy Farms
George Baker, Loyalsock

I grew up in Martinsburg, near Altoona, and spent much of my time as a youth working on a farm. After high school I studied agriculture at Penn State and was hired by the Farmers Home Administration right after college. Following a short stint in Towanda, I came to Williamsport where I worked for FHA for over thirty years, giving advice and lending money to Lycoming County farmers.

Of course, the U.S. government doesn't lend money to every farmer. When a farmer needed money, we had to understand why, and this meant a visit to the farm and an analysis of his problem. We wouldn't throw good money after a failing venture, or bankroll a problem that would only get worse. If a farmer had poor milk production and we found ten sick cows, we wanted him to cull those cows before we loaned him money. With a good herd, he could pay back his loan. Of the hundreds of farms I visited over the years, most of them went bust and a whole way of life went with them. Farms that remained grew bigger, more mechanized, more scientific, and more efficient. I want to talk a bit about what went on in dairy farming during the years I worked in Williamsport, from around 1945 to 1975.

In 1976 I completed a study of dairy farming in

Lycoming County. At that time FHA showed only
two hundred sixty remaining farms. Yet in 1958 we
had eight hundred dairy farms, and before that over
a thousand. What happened to all those small
family-run dairy farms in central Pennsylvania?
During my years at FHA, I had watched the demise
of these small farms and asked myself what was going
on. Back in the thirties and forties, people thought
the best place in the world was a farm. Young
women wanted to marry farmers, boys dreamed of
owning their own farms. And the small farm *was* a
wonderful place. Everything fresh and growing, lots
of good things to eat, little need for cash, no Great
Depression, no time clock to punch. You could get
by on twenty-five hundred dollars a year and support
an entire family. Eighty acres and twenty or thirty
cows was all you needed. Everything was fine until
after the war.

By the 1950s the small farmers knew they weren't
going to make it. First, the government redefined
what it meant by a farm. In short, the new FHA
lending laws favored the bigger farms, while money
grew tighter for the small farmers. Furthermore, to
live decently in modern America, you needed
money, a substantial income. On the new dairy farm
you needed tractors, automatic milkers and a milking
parlor, automatic spreaders, silos, combines, bulk
tanks, and more. Gone were the days of barter and
low cash on a small farm. The small farmer saw
poverty staring him in the face. To give you an
example of what I am talking about, think of this:
the Amish have moved in and bought up some small
dairy farms in Lycoming County and by their

standards they are thriving. Why? Because they live by nineteenth-century standards. They don't need electricity, cars, lots of clothes, and college educations. But the small farmers back in the 1950s wanted the goods of our society and found they couldn't afford them.

Suddenly they could see that to survive they had to grow, and to grow they needed to borrow lots of money. They came to FHA. Of course, we knew what was happening long before they did. We knew the surviving dairy farms would be large, mechanized, and scientifically efficient. For a small farmer to go big he would have to borrow a hundred to two hundred thousand dollars right off the bat. Well, most of the traditional farmers just said no. They couldn't see that. It was crazy, made no sense. But a few smart, brave souls went and borrowed the money and managed it well. Today they are the successful, big farmers in the county, men like Harold Drick and John Bower over in Elimsport, Dick Bardo in Muncy, and the Doebler family in Jersey Shore.

People have asked me why didn't the farmers ban together, form co-ops, share machinery and labor? I can't give a better answer than to say it just isn't in the nature of a farmer to form a union or a co-op. He is an independent cuss, competitive, suspicious, and used to doing things his way. Here's a few examples: Sullivan County was once big potato country, hundreds of farms all over. A few years ago, my wife and I visited an isolated Catholic church outside New Albany, and all around for miles lay the stone fences and cellars of abandoned potato farms—

all gone. Anyway, the potato farmers decided to pool their machinery and labor by forming co-ops—a hundred and sixty of them, but they just couldn't work it out. They lasted a few years at best and today are all gone. When a crop is ready, a farmer wants to harvest it today; he does not want to wait until his neighbor finishes with his combine or plow.

Another example of what held the farmer back was tradition—a good thing in itself, but dangerous at the time of this change. Farmers had done things one way for generations, and they just couldn't bring themselves to change. Take oats, for example. Farmers loved to grow oats because their fathers and grandfathers grew oats. So we showed them scientific studies proving oats yielded the least nutrition per acre of any crop, and silage corn yielded by far the most. Still, they were reluctant to change.

Small dairy farmers grew so fond of their cows they kept them even when their production dropped. When they came to FHA for a loan, we'd order a study of their herd by the Herd Improvement Association to measure milk production over a month. Usually the study would show they needed to cull eight unproductive cows. Then we'd say we would lend money for new cows if the old cows went. You see, on the modern, highly productive dairy farm, the cows turn over about every five years. Well, these farmers would say, "Oh, no, that's ole Jane and Bobbie and Bossie, I just can't let them go."

It was sad to see, but when you went to the successful farms, you could see the change was inevitable. Farmers like Bower, Drick, and Bardo were the best farmers I ever saw. They ran large farms efficiently, milking over a hundred head and keeping their machinery costs down. That was the key: keeping the quality of the herd up and the cost of machinery down. The Doebler family would clean and oil their machinery and store it right after its final use each year. In spring, when most farmers start cleaning their equipment, their harvesters and tractors look like new. They sell about fifteen percent of the seed corn in Pennsylvania and they run a marvelous operation.

During the fifties and sixties, the Farmers Home Administration often had to turn down the loan applications of small farmers precisely because they wouldn't or couldn't change. Using the right fertilizer was often a big problem. Now, the important elements in farm soil generally are nitrogen, phosphorus, and potash. Farmers were used to applying a tried-and-true fertilizer called" five-ten-ten," meaning five percent nitrogen and so on. But soil analysis, if we could get them to do it, would often show a soil needing fifteen percent nitrogen. The old fertilizer clearly wouldn't do, but the farmer had his ways and wouldn't change, so FHA couldn't help him. Soon another farm would go under.

For pure production, big farms work better and keep the cost of milk down for the consumer. Dairy farms you see today are survivors run by smart, daring families. They juggle about a million dollars' worth of stock and property against a quarter-million-dollar debt and a hundred-thousand-dollar milk bill. But I have seen hundreds of small family farms in Lycoming County go out of business. It makes a man sad. Small dairy farms once covered our valleys, bustling homesteads with cows, chickens, and children coloring the hillsides. Now these farms have faded into woods, grown over with sumac and briar, caved in, silent, and forgotten.

Earthmover
Chester "Shorty" Goodwin, Holliday

That's Baker Hollow behind us, and our house sits on the rise here looking on the town of Holliday and Crooked Creek. In the distance you can see the new Hammond Lake. We've got bears, coons, deer, rattlers, beavers, muskrats, a few minks, turkeys, and coyotes up Baker Hollow. Fact is, I'm on my way to trap some coyotes for a friend who's got sheep. I built my trapping cabin away from the house like this to cut down on scent. See all my traps hanging there? There's beaver, muskrat, and fox traps. I get my limit of six beaver every year. We chinked the cabin with oakum; the logs were from trees planted when I was a teenager over on the family property, so they're over fifty years old.

I was born in 1921 in Wellsboro Junction, but we soon moved to a three-hundred-sixty-acre farm in Niles Valley. We milked about twenty-five cows by hand and made a living, I recall. Out there, boys learned to hunt and fish early. We caught suckers, eels, trout, turtles, and frogs and ate them all. Though the deer were few, the rabbits and squirrels were plentiful. You hardly ever saw a deer back then.

Rattlesnakes turned up all over the place. In one twenty-acre field on my father's farm, we killed twenty-one rattlesnakes. One day I saw my father pitch up a rattlesnake with some hay onto the haycock. The hired man let out a scream and jumped off the wagon. Two of my friends got bit and didn't die. One summer day we were all playing baseball on the field at Holliday when the batter hit a hard line drive to Homer Lion in center field. Homer ran for the ball and suddenly stopped and stood just staring at the ground. We all ran out, and there was a big old timber rattler swallowing a rabbit, just laying there and working those jaws. I killed two of them right out back last summer. Now, the folks who want to preserve the rattler—well, we should mail them the snakes . . . let them crawl around in *their* yards.

When I was twelve, I started fixing and operating machines in Joe Borden's store. I have always gotten my greatest satisfaction from fixing a diesel or a 'dozer or an airplane that nobody else could fix. When three mechanics come to me and say, "Shorty, we can't fix it, but we know you can," then I'm happy. Sure, I'll fix it, but I won't tell you what was wrong or just what I did—that's my secret. When I was working for Jones and Bragg in the strippings, I fixed a loader one night with my crew— tore it all down and made it work like new. Couple of years later, I got a call from West Virginia—see, they'd sent the loader down there—and the mechanics wanted to know how I fixed it, but I wouldn't tell them.

When I wasn't fixing heavy machinery, I was running it. During much of World War II, I worked as flight engineer for an air rescue plane stationed in Hawaii. Later in the war, I was master mechanic up in Newfoundland, supervising the draining of a swamp in a location where they were building two big gun emplacements. Well, I was digging with the blade of my dozer down about three feet when suddenly I came up with two sections of a five-inch cable in my bucket. I had just cut through the Transatlantic Telephone Cable! It didn't take long for lots of people to arrive. Soon we dug another, deeper ditch and spliced a new section into the cable.

After the war, I worked in New York State building roads and moving earth. I preferred to work at night because with the lights on you can only see what you're working on, you're not distracted. You just do your job. Sometimes I would work on the concrete crews laying the new highways. Twenty years ago, we laid concrete for a mile of single-lane highway in one day. That was considered a great accomplishment. A few years before I retired, we laid a mile of two-lane concrete highway in less than a day. All the highway machines are so much bigger today.

Working in the strip mines is always the same every day. I would operate a dozer cleaning up after the drag line or building roads. Some companies made me wear a special belt to track the dust in the air. Had to wear it all day and turn it in at night. Of course, the fellows in the mines got black lung bad. I know men who could barely breathe. Of course, I say if you're gonna get it you're gonna get it. They collect a good benefit from black lung, though.

Safety first, I always say. When I got hurt a few years ago, it ended my working life. How did it happen? I was putting a differential in a ten-yard loader—you know the big round ball where an axle and drive shaft come together on a truck. Well, this one was very big. We were using the bucket on a 'dozer to lift up the axle of the truck. While the dozer was holding the truck frame up in the air, I went underneath the frame to bolt things together. Now, while I was underneath her screwing the cover back on the gears, suddenly the hydraulic cables broke on the 'dozer and the bucket lost all power. I felt the truck frame fall on my back. It pushed me into the ground, I could feel blood running out of my eyes, ears, nose, and mouth; I could see blood pooling on the ground. Then I passed out. They got me out with a portable jack. It was ten days before I really came to and knew what had happened. When the frame fell, it split my pelvis, broke my knee and my ankle. One of my kidneys was crushed. I sat there bawling in the hospital because I knew I'd have to retire. But, you know, I'm still running a trap line, still hunting and fishing, and I built this cabin last year.

Now I want to tell you about the years I spent in Saudi Arabia—twelve of 'em—working for the oil company. They sent me there to fix the heavy equipment and to teach the Saudis how to tear down and rebuild engines. I even studied Arabic for six weeks. I got along fine with the Saudis. They had a funny way of looking at things. Everything was the will of Allah. Now, one time my men were working an oil rig with a whip line. That was a cable we could shoot up to the top of the rig to pull up pipe quickly because we had a whole mile of pipe underground. So one day one of the Arabs grabs hold of the whip line as it starts to shoot up and just hoods on and zip—up he goes about sixty feet in the air, never saying a word. Immediately we started to lower it, but when it is twenty feet off the ground he loses his grip and falls—splat on the deck.

"Why did you hang on to the whip line, I asked?"

Well, he just looked at me wide-eyed and said, "God told me to come."

See, that was their answer for almost anything. Allah had willed it. "En Shalla," they would say.

I'm sixty-eight this year. I've had a fine life, and I don't think there's much that I would change if I could. I've worked on big projects all over the world and all over the country. I'm proud of what I've accomplished. Today when Thelma and I are riding around with one of our grandchildren and we hit a bumpy stretch of the highway, the kids will say, "Grandma, did Grandpa build this stretch of road?"

Thelma will just laugh and say, "Of course, he did."

The Woods Kid Who Became a Forester
Dick Sassaman, Sterling Run

I grew up a woods kid, hunting, fingering trout, and chasing snakes. I wouldn't go across the street to play baseball or football. I ran with the big kids, knew where they hid cigarettes and beer when I was eight.

When I was about seven, I got in trouble with my parents. I had done something very wrong, though I can't remember what. Anyway, after they bawled me out, I just looked at them and said, "You know, I could leave this house right now, and I know some places where you you'd *never* find me."

Of course, to this day they have never let me forget that, but it was true. I lived in a world of secret bear caves and brook trout streams, abandoned dynamite factories, and never-visited hollows and mountaintops. Cameron County may be wild today, but fifty years ago it was very wild. We used to be a big dynamite producer because of the sheltered hollows. I can remember five of six dynamite factories around Emporium. The last factory of the Pennsylvania Powder Company blew up in 1957 right where Mallory's Sawmill stands today outside Emporium. That terrific nighttime blast brought everybody in the county right out of their beds and killed three men. That was the last of the dynamite.

We used to roam the deserted West Branch of the Susquehanna around Karthus when I was older. Our favorite game was catching rattlesnakes. We had broken-off car antennas that telescoped out, and on the narrow tip we soldered turtle hooks. We prowled the old lumber camps with their huge bark piles—a favorite snake place. Forty or fifty snakes would start buzzin' as we approached, and we'd quick reach down between the bark piles, hook a rattler, and flip him out. We'd get about six apiece before the rest slid under the bark. We'd kill 'em or take some home for pets, or eat them—sort of a tough chicken they tasted like. Over there is my trophy for first place in

the State Rattlesnake Sacking at Sinnemahoning a
few years ago. Yeah, I've been bitten but only by a
dry hit—the snake had no venom at the time.

After high school I went to automotive school and
worked for a time in the local car dealership, but my
love for the outdoors was so strong I wanted to go
into forestry. I attended Lycoming College for two
years, went to Forest Rangers School in New York
State and began working in the State Forestry Office
here in Emporium as a forest technician over twenty-
five years ago. I do a bit of everything in this job and
I like it.

Between St. Marys and Emporium and extending
about thirty miles south you have about two hundred
square miles of forest that make up the range of the
Pennsylvania elk herd. Today this herd consists of
about a hundred thirty-five animals; forty years ago, it
was down to only about twenty animals. In 1867 the
last native elk was killed near Ridgway, Pennsylvania,
along the headwaters of the Clarion River, a few miles
from here. Around 1920 the Game Commission began
stocking elk from Yellowstone and other western parks
in Cameron and Elk counties. They succeeded in
establishing a western species of elk where the eastern
species had once flourished. Today I am deeply
involved with the elk herd. It is my hobby, my passion.
We are involved in tracking, darting, tagging, and
monitoring the herd. Once each year in January—
because we can see them better in snow—we count the
herd by helicopter as well as from the ground. We get
to within one or two of the actual number of elk on the
entire range, about ninety-eight percent accurate.

The enemies to our herd are man, brainworm, and

wild dogs. Just the other day, someone shot a bull and a pregnant cow. That kind of thing happens every year. People get wild and just start shooting. One guy actually shot an elk right in front of a bunch of people. Farmers can shoot the elk for crop damage, but they cannot collect on crop damage from elk. Farmers know the elk meat tastes good, so they always shoot the bull, never the cow. Only a few elk get killed that way, though.

Last year, wild dogs killed a cow and her calf, which is kind of unusual. It isn't unusual for them to kill the calf, but usually the cow will hold them off and then get away. Of course, people have no idea how many dogs can run in one of these packs. I've seen as many as twelve, and they aren't afraid of anything. That's where the danger lies: a domesticated animal gone wild just doesn't know fear. That's why this new breed of coydogs will soon get out of hand—it's part coyote, part dog. Mixed breeds will become more efficient predators. It's the dog in them that frightens me. The dog isn't afraid of anything. We've seen a real increase in the coyote population up here.

Brainworm is a long stringy worm that travels to the elk's brain from its digestive system. The deer have brainworm too, but it leaves their brain to lay eggs in the deer's stomach, so the eggs come out in the deer's feces. Then snails eat the eggs, and in turn the elk eat the tiny snails when they eat grass. That is the cycle. An elk with brainworm walks with a stagger or wobble. Sometimes when they fall they can't get up again. We've gone up and petted them. The horns of a sick bull get all twisted. One female we call "the sick cow" has all the symptoms, wobbles around, and has lived on for about six years. Most bulls with brainworm look haggard, emaciated, and drunk. Their racks grow twisted. Eventually they die. We manhandled one into captivity and trucked it down to the University of Pennsylvania where they found a positive infection of brainworm. Dangerous as it is, we know brainworm isn't a limiting factor on the elk herd. It only affects a few individuals a year. We have such a small herd we have to be very careful.

Management of the elk herd is a cooperative project shared by the State Game Commission and the Bureau of Forestry. I've spent a good deal of time darting, banding, and tracking the elk. Several times when we were moving an animal I have come close to getting crushed. Oddly enough, tourists do not drive here in great numbers to see these magnificent animals. However, many people in this region know where to find the elk, especially when the grasses are in. Off Route 555, midway between Driftwood and Weedville, is a place called Benezette where the bulls go to meet the cows during the fall mating season. Here a large grassy plain makes for good grazing and good elk-watching during the summer and early fall. Elk also cluster at nearby Winslow Hill where a reclaimed strip mine offers good grazing.

Animal life ebbs and flows in the big woods. Today we see golden eagles, mostly at the deer dump where we drop the road kills. We're starting to see bobcats again, big ones up to forty pounds, and different kinds of owls, like the solwet, usually a more northern bird. The Pennsylvania bear has been reproducing better than any other species, so they're all over the place. The white-tail, according to the Game Commission, has overpopulated. International Paper owns thousands of acres around here. They felt they had a deer problem—too many seedlings eaten—so they got the bright idea of posting and then renting out their land to hunters. Of course, the problem got worse. They should have just opened up their land for everyone to hunt. That's what I call pooping in your own mess kit.

I have always lived in the country. When I drive on the Cross Bronx Expressway in New York City, I feel like I'm having a heart attack. I don't know how people can live that way. I've had a good life here so far: my two sons are in the United States Air Force Academy, the elk herd is healthier than its been in fifty years, and I've got a job that lets me move around the mountains in every season. Look around you. I've hunted almost everything on this continent, I've hiked to places where almost no one has been, and I've been able to observe wildlife almost every day of my life. What more could a man want?